MORE
ADVENTIST
HOT
POTATOES

Legalistic
Education

Nature
of Christ

Independent
Ministries

Health
System

Martin Weber

Pacific Press Publishing Association
Boise, Idaho
Oshawa, Ontario, Canada

Edited by Marvin Moore and Russell Holt
Designed by Dennis Ferree
Cover illustration by Lars Justinen
Typeset in 10/12 Century Schoolbook

Scripture references are taken from the New King James
Version unless otherwise noted.

The author is responsible for the accuracy of all quotations
except for those from Scripture.

Library of Congress Cataloging-in-Publication Data:

Weber, Martin, 1951-
  More Adventist hot potatoes: legalistic education, independ-
ent ministries, nature of Christ / Martin Weber.
      p.   cm.
    ISBN 0-8163-1090-4
    1. Seventh-day Adventists—Doctrines. 2. Adventists—
Doctrines. 3. Sabbatarians—Doctrines.   I. Title.
BX6154.W4225   1992
286.7'32—dc20   91-45290
                                                      CIP

92 93 94 95 96 · 5 4 3 2 1

MORE
ADVENTIST
HOT
POTATOES

Contents

Dedication

To my precious wife, Darlene,
I dedicate this book.
Her unfailing patience
made it possible,
and her tender love
brightens every day.

Introduction

More Hot Potatoes?

The story is told of a young preacher, fresh out of Bible school, who wanted to impress his little Kentucky church about how strongly he stood against sin. His first Sunday he preached against the evils of smoking. After the sermon, the old deacon came over and whispered, "You'd better look out, son. One-third of these folks are tobacco farmers."

Strike one.

The next Sunday the young man spoke out against the evils of drinking. The deacon, looking quite irritated, took him aside again. "Young feller, don't you know one-third of us here are in the bourbon business?"

Strike two.

The third Sunday the young man condemned with conviction the evils of gambling. You guessed it—the remnant of his audience raised thoroughbred horses for the racetracks.

Strike three.

The irate board members called an emergency meeting to rid themselves of their tormentor, the one who dared to disturb business as usual. The desperate young man realized that his convictions weren't getting him anywhere but out the door. He begged the church to give him one more chance.

The next Sunday he preached his most powerful sermon yet to that Kentucky congregation. Waving his arms with authority, he damned the evils of deep-sea fishing outside the boundaries of international waters!

From then on he had smooth sailing. Everybody loved him. Finally the young preacher had learned the lesson of political survival: Don't let your convictions get you in trouble. In whatever you say and whatever you do, keep everybody happy. Go ahead and speak out against sin—but not the sins your audience is guilty of.

Politically speaking, I guess I've struck out from time to time in my ministry, even though I'm a people pleaser by nature. I'll do anything to keep people from getting angry, except if I hear the gospel being blasphemed or our church slandered. Then I feel compelled to speak out and be heard. Whatever the political risk, I feel I should plunge right in and try to rescue sincere souls from being deceived by legalism, liberalism, or anything else the devil tries to drown us in.

If your conscience is troubled about something— anything—let's talk. I might be able to help you find peace of mind and freedom from guilt. If you think I'm mistaken, try to help me; I take all criticism seriously. But if you only want to argue with me, count me out.

In my first *Hot Potatoes* book, there wasn't room for all the things we needed to discuss. Hence this sequel. The potatoes here are just as hot as the ones before, just as controversial—like the chapters on the Adventist Health System, independent ministries, and our educational system.

You may wonder what qualifies me to analyze the health system. I wondered about that too. So I asked the advice of a friend who is president of one of our hospitals.

"Martin," he replied, "many Adventists have lost confidence in our health system. They've heard all kinds of bad news about us, some of which is true and some of which isn't. That chapter of yours *needs* to be written, and you're the one to do it."

"How's that?" I wanted to know.

"You've got no vested interest—no turf to protect, no ax to grind. You can say things I would like to say, but can't. You love the church, and you'll be fair. Just do thorough research and keep your facts straight. Most of us will appreciate it."

With that word, I went ahead and prepared this book. Please keep the following in mind as you read these pages:

- My goal is not to raise doubts but to settle them.
- I'm not so arrogant or ignorant as to imagine I have

8

all the answers. I'm just trying to foster a balanced understanding of matters about which consciences are troubled.

• I recognize—and I hope you do too—that there's room in the Seventh-day Adventist Church for differing convictions on many things. Certain pillars of faith define us as a movement, and we must support them together in preserving our unique identity. But remember, we are not a cult that forces all members to goose-step along in mindless uniformity like Hitler's storm troopers. Regarding certain disputable questions of conscience, the Lord declares, "Let each be fully convinced in his own mind." "So then each of us shall give account of himself to God" (Romans 14:5, 12).

• Those newly released from the bondage of legalism sometimes dispense with Christian standards altogether. That's tragic, but you know how human nature tends to swing like a pendulum from one extreme to another. To safeguard against that, I fervently exalt the law of God as the test of our relationship with Christ. Please don't blame me if someone disregards my cautions and brings disgrace upon the grace of God. I think any fair-minded person who reads my books recognizes that I denounce sinful indulgence in any form.

All God's gifts can be abused or taken to extreme. Should we stop bringing food to famished people because some will kill themselves by abusing the lifesaving gift? Then let's not stop offering the lifegiving grace of God, despite the potential for permissiveness.

• Many of the problems covered in this book concern the Adventist Church in North America more than in South and Central America and other parts of the world. Although I've visited many countries, ministering in several of them, I feel qualified at this point to analyze our situation only in North America.

• Keep in mind that I'm not writing this book as the official voice of the church or any of its institutions or leaders. What you read here are my personal opinions, formed by my own research and discussion. If you don't like what you read here, blame me and me alone.

• As important as it is to know the truth on these vital matters, it is equally important to maintain a spirit of Christian love.

I also think I need to ask your forgiveness. When writing my book *Adventist Hot Potatoes*, in several places I was not as kind as I should have been, particularly in the chapter "Sister Stern." I poked fun at her obstinate legalism, saying she was "constipated with guilt." I also said that her idea of a big evening was to retire early and turn the electric blanket up to medium.

Very descriptive, very clever, but not very nice. I'm sorry.

The message of that chapter is exceedingly important, and I really did try to be careful in how I wrote *Hot Potatoes*. Basically, I think I succeeded in steering clear of sarcasm—except for several paragraphs. Let's see if I can avoid anything caustic in this book.

I hope instead that in these pages you'll find the mercy and truth of Jesus Christ sprinkled tastefully on each of our hot potatoes. I want you to enjoy this meal I've prepared. If you find yourself getting indigestion—and you think it's my fault—do me a favor and let me know.

Chapter 1

Christian Education Is Not Child Sacrifice

(Adventist Education)

"You're an ugly freckle-faced——! Not only that, you dress stupid and you walk funny. You are a total jerk. We all hate you. We wish you would get lost."

So went the little note of encouragement and affirmation passed to the sixth-grade daughter of a friend of mine. It came to her because she stood up for a fellow classmate who had suffered ridicule week after week to the point that she wanted to quit church school. The wrath of the oppressors then turned on her helper.

When the father of the recipient saw the note, he determined to withdraw his daughter from the school. His wife, though equally incensed, disagreed. "This school was ordained by God!" she declared. "We can never abandon it."

"Seems to me the Lord has already abandoned that place," he retorted. "It's not just this incident—so many things like it happen every week. And that filthy language on the playground whenever the teachers aren't around! Public schools could hardly be worse. I believe in Christian education, but not child sacrifice."

The situation was resolved when the mother showed the note to the principal. The student who wrote it received a three-day suspension, and life returned to normal.

Upon hearing of the incident, I thanked the principal for her prompt and firm response. And then I got to thinking. Was the victim's father justified in assessing that our schools are not that different from those of the world? How much are teachers responsible for whatever problems we have, and how much should parents bear the blame? What's wrong with Adventist education—and what's right about it?

Before attempting this analysis, I want to affirm my enthusiastic support for Adventist education. The remarkable success of our church throughout the world is largely due to our educational system. All my life through college I've attended our schools. It was in a week of prayer at Columbia Union College that I accepted Christ one brisk October evening. During my first pastorate in a poor Appalachian conference, our little group established a one-room church school. To help fund that school, my wife and I returned a quarter of our salary to the church, putting off the purchase of a much-needed car (which the Lord supplied us anyway). After accepting a pastorate in California, I served on an academy board and recently participated in a spiritual evaluation project for the local church school.

So you see, I've been intimately involved with Adventist education from my childhood. All my observations and suggestions in this chapter come from a heart that loves and supports our schools.

We Adventists need to thank the Lord for the school system He has helped us to establish. We operate more than 5,000 schools in 142 nations. These schools employ more than 35,000 teachers, and enrollment stands at nearly three-quarters of a million students. Our school system is the largest education program sponsored by a single Protestant denomination.[1]

Aren't you glad for a church that takes seriously the training of its young people? Surprisingly, perhaps, education has not always played an important role in our church. First came the establishment of a strong publishing work. Then came the organization of our conference structure, followed by our health-care program. Finally, with a big boost from Ellen White, our church was prepared to address the importance of taking care of its young people. Ellen White's publication of *Christian Education* in 1893 laid the groundwork for our present school system.

George Akers, a former director of the Education Department

of the General Conference, applies the counsel of Ellen White to our present situation:

> The primary mission of a Christian school is to produce Christians—and in our case Christians who are thoroughly grounded in historic Adventism.
>
> Second, it endeavors to provide our children and youth with quality basic education so that they might effectively cope with their world.
>
> At the college and university level, it undertakes to prepare professionals for service to the world church.[2]

Dr. Akers continues: "The real measure of a school is what is happening to students there. That is, what kind of mind-set is ... the institution developing in its students? One that is selfish, secular, and materialistic? Or one that is deeply spiritual—centered on God?"[3]

Such is the divine mandate for our school system. How well are we fulfilling it?

Last autumn a phone call came from a good friend, Thearon Staddon. He shared the news that his teenage son Jack had just won a state scholastic championship sponsored by the National Geographic Society. Jack was going on to represent Nebraska in the national championship. A few weeks later I got a call from the excited young man himself, telling me what I had already read in *USA Today*. He had won first prize in the national competition, to the glory of God and the praise of the Adventist school system.

Jack's younger brother Jeff is no slouch, either. After the Staddon family moved to fill a pastorate in the state of Washington, Jeff placed second in the same competition there. (He actually deserved to win the grand prize, but the official scorekeeper apparently became confused about one contestant's answer to a crucial question.)

Jack and Jeff Staddon represent the finest in Christian education. Both of them are brilliant scholastically while also deeply committed to God. They are living evidence that the quality of scholarship in our schools continues to rise. My church-school education, I have to say, was decidedly inferior to what my children now receive. While there is always room for more improvement, I believe that overall we earn an A or a B-plus for our scholastics.

One challenge is to help our teachers' paychecks keep pace with the increased salaries of the public schools. We expect our teachers to be professionals, and we ought to pay them adequately, not taking unfair advantage of their dedicated service.

So much for maintaining a good academic standard. Spiritually, how do we measure up? Perhaps the best grade we can give ourselves is a C. The results vary from one student to the next, but we must all acknowledge that most of them have a hard time rising above the general spiritual malaise known as Laodicea that afflicts many Seventh-day Adventists in North America.

I am sure that part of the problem lies in the homes our children come from. Dr. Akers suggests this:

> If the family's lifestyle is worldly (particularly with respect to unregulated television viewing), the children and youth who attend church school are thrown into spiritual chaos. They find themselves living in two different worlds, each with its own value system. This produces a state of suspension and internal conflict. Many of them do not survive this battle, becoming mere numbers in the church's youth attrition statistics.[4]

However, beyond the problems in the home, we cannot deny that there are also flaws in our school system. Teachers are not perfect, and sometimes they make mistakes that hurt our children. There are stories of hypocrisy. I recall hearing about a teacher who lectured her class on the virtues of vegetarianism, only to go to a local fast-food restaurant and order a hamburger. There are stories of partiality, lack of fairness, and incompetence. I personally know of instances of abuse—physical, emotional, and even sexual—among Adventist teachers. We live in an imperfect and sinful world, and it is inevitable that those who operate our schools will sometimes be imperfect and sinful.

I can understand why those whose children are hurt by these

imperfections question the value of Christian education. If our schools routinely encouraged these problems, we would be compelled to concur with their concerns. But I am convinced that for every problem teacher there are a dozen who are competent and compassionate.

I thank God for the bright spots during my years in our schools. I think of my fifth-grade teacher, Miss Elsie Steuer, who sacrificed a well-paying position in the public-school system to join our newly formed consolidated school. From her meager salary she paid the entire tuition charge for my brothers and me. That dear woman must share some credit for whatever I might accomplish in life.

As I think back on my church-school experience, unfortunately, I must admit that Elsie Steuer's compassion seemed like a scarce commodity in our classrooms. Some teachers didn't seem to understand young people. I felt as though they interpreted every act of attention-getting mischief as rebellion against God, and their remedy for this childish misbehavior was a daily dose of guilt from the throne of grace. They told us that Jesus would take only "perfect" children to heaven. Our week-of-prayer speakers reminded us that probation was about to close and that we needed to be "good enough" to make it without a Mediator.

Those are my memories of church school and academy back in the 1960s. From what I can see today in my travels around the North American Division, our educational system has changed dramatically. Much of the legalism has been purged from our Bible class textbooks. Only a minority of teachers these days major in guilt and fear. They are generally less harsh and more sensitive to the self-esteem of their students. Conference educational directors work hard to foster emotional growth and positive relationships in the classroom.

Unfortunately, most people I talk with believe that the level of spirituality in our schools is not keeping pace with other improvements. Strict legalism has given way, not to spiritual fervor, but to laxity and liberalism. In many areas of North America, our young people don't seem concerned about facing God's judgment. Few of them seem bothered by guilt as they emerge from the shopping malls sporting their new designer outfits. Nevertheless, their comprehension of God's grace remains woefully anemic. A recent article in *Ministry* magazine reported some disappointing results from a survey of 12,000 Adventist youth: 62 percent said that "the way to be accepted by God is to try sincerely to live a good life."[5]

Evidently, underneath our laxity and liberalism is a foundation of what you might call "loose legalism." It doesn't burden the conscience as strict legalism did a generation ago, but neither does it fill the heart with joyous assurance in Christ. A humanistic, materialistic paralysis afflicts many if not most of our schools. Our commitment to behavioral standards seems superficial, "having the form of godliness but denying the power thereof."

Many of today's teachers are from my generation, burned out from the rigors of an unpleasant and unloving religious upbringing. Having escaped the bondage of fanaticism, are they now wandering in the spacious but barren desert of secularism? Whatever the reason for the lack of spirituality among many of our teachers, we cannot deny that our schools need a revival of genuine godliness just as much now as in the old days of suffocating legalism.

Adventist young people also need a lot more love from the adults of the church. As I mentioned, many of our teachers are really trying to enhance self-worth and acceptance, yet surveys continue to remind us that the church is failing to provide a friendly and accepting atmosphere. It's tragic but true—many of our young people feel that older Adventists don't really care about them.

That sad reality is documented by the Valuegenesis project, a major survey of nearly 13,000 North American Adventists. As reported in the *Adventist Review*, just 57 percent of our youth expressed agreement with the following statement: "My teachers or adult leaders care about me."[6] In contrast, Valuegenesis reveals that 84 percent of Southern Baptist youth believe their teachers and leaders care about them.

Sixty-two percent of Baptist youth responded favorably to this statement: "I experience the feeling that adults [in general] in my local church care about me." Regrettably, only 29 percent of Adventist youth in North America could say that the adults of their church care about them. In other words, 71 percent of our young people feel that we adults *don't* really like them.

Doesn't this break your heart?

Someone may be thinking, "Well, at least we Adventists obey the law of God."

Really? The Bible says, "Love does no harm to its neighbor; therefore love is the fulfillment of the law" (Romans 13:10). When the majority of our young people don't feel loved by the adults of the church, our so-called "law keeping" only does more harm than good. The Valuegenesis survey proves it.

That same survey indicates that only 36 percent of Adventist youth look forward to going to church, whereas 76 percent of Baptist youth do. And 31 percent of Adventist young people say that "religious education programs at my church are interesting"; but 74 percent of Baptist youth enjoy their religious education.[7]

Thank God, the news is not all bad. Seventy percent of Adventist youth proclaimed loyalty to their church.[8] The question must be asked, however, Is this loyalty a social commitment to the Adventist culture, or do these youth have a genuine spiritual commitment to Christ? The fact is that among seniors attending Adventist academies, the Valuegenesis survey indicates that "less than one in five have developed both a high faith maturity and high loyalty to the Adventist Church."[9]

If you have any questions about that, I suggest you conduct your own informal survey. Just pick up the yearbook from your local academy and flip through the pages. Find the section where students list their likes and dislikes, their hopes and dreams. How much do you read about love for Jesus and desire to help lost souls be saved for His soon coming? Most of what you see will probably be depressingly secular.

Let's be honest. A registration application for church school is not a ticket to heaven. The fact is that in most of our North American schools, from coast to coast, it just isn't considered "cool" to be religious. Not that our young people are bad; it's just that they are so secular. Most of them wouldn't dare get excited about Jesus, lest their peers accuse them of "kissing up" to the religious establishment represented by their teachers.

MORE ADVENTIST HOT POTATOES

What a contrast is our spiritual situation with those parts of the world where soul-winning academies and colleges light up Mission Spotlight reports. Because we love our polished and professional educational system in North America and Australia, it's easy to become blindly defensive. But true loyalty doesn't deny reality. Without condemning anyone, we must confront our deficiencies. Our Lord calls us to "be zealous . . . and repent" (Revelation 3:19).

Let's not get discouraged, though. There is much going on with Adventist youth that we can rejoice in. The Valuegenesis survey indicates that our schools, despite their problems, do have positive spiritual influences at work within them. Many shining stars among our teachers light up Adventist classrooms. Hardly have I seen a school that doesn't have at least one faculty member with a strong spiritual commitment springing from a heart of joy and love. A number of academies, and even some elementary schools, sponsor soul-winning and community compassion projects. All our colleges have expanded their local and international student missionary programs.

I know personally of a school that provides students opportunities to share Christ's love and fulfill the gospel commission. Faculty members personally train young people in giving Bible studies and other evangelism projects. I've heard marvelous reports of how many students are really on fire for the Lord in that school.

Because of schools like this one—and we have many fine academies and colleges—I believe that Christian education is certainly worth our financial sacrifice. I *definitely would not* want to put my children at risk in public schools. Evolution propaganda I'm not particularly concerned about; my family has been grounded in belief about a creator God, and I can handle on a day-by-day basis any questions that could come up. I'm more worried about the social structure revolving around dances and Friday-night football games. And what really frightens me about public schools is sex education.

In the wisdom of the world, fornication with "protection" is responsible behavior. There are no absolutes to govern behavior. Abortion is not a matter of morality. Homosexuality is a perfectly legitimate option. Such is the daily bombardment of secular humanism suffered by students in the public educational system.

Because sex is such a powerful force, how can we willingly entrust our adolescents to a school that would steer them astray? Our teenagers need a moral foundation that only a Bible-based educational system can supply.

How about your local Baptist school? They do teach Christian morality there, but you would still have a Sabbath social problem—compounded by an emphasis on Sunday church attendance. Then there's the teaching of eternal hell and other unscriptural doctrines.

No, thanks. Our children and youth need an *Adventist* Christian education.

But suppose your local academy has been hijacked by liberalism or legalism. Should you send them there anyway?

Again, let me be honest. The Adventist educational system is not perfect. However, the imperfection is not spread evenly across the board. Just as each individual is different from every other individual, so each school is different from every other school. Some of our schools are excellent, while others have serious flaws. I believe it is the parents' responsibility to evaluate the available options and enroll their children in the school they consider to be the very best, even if it means sending them 1,000 miles away from home.

If I found myself employed by a conference that required me to enroll my son and daughter in an academy that I knew would threaten their souls, I would take that as a sign that God wanted me to leave that conference. Under God, my family must come first, especially their spiritual welfare. What shall it profit a minister if he baptizes the whole city but loses his own precious children?

Many parents tell me that switching academies has done wonders for their teenagers. The change of environment is just what they needed to orient themselves spiritually and socially.

However, if the best academy is beyond daily commuting distance, think carefully before transplanting a fourteen-year-old from the security of the family circle to a dorm setting, especially if the young person is insecure or unusually impressionable. An adolescent may survive such an arrangement, but I've seen too many of them led astray by peers even in the best of Christian schools. On the other hand, moving the family might bring tremendous hardship and may in fact be impossible. To me, the bottom line is this: While it is best for young teenagers to live at home, dorm life in a really good academy is usually an acceptable option. It certainly seems better than exposing them to the bombardment of sexual temptation in the typical public school or the laxity or legalism in some local academies.

Each situation is different. God will lead you as you trust Him for guidance.

Now the question, How do you select the best Christian academy or college for your teenager? What's the best way to check around?

It would be too much to expect objective counsel from faculty members or conference educational directors. They are understandably biased in favor of the schools they represent. Instead, talk with other parents and their teenagers who have had experiences with different schools. Counsel with pastors who might know. After you have narrowed down the list of possible schools, invest a few weekends and visit several schools yourself. Get to know the faculty, especially the dormitory deans, the Bible teachers, and the principal. Do they really seem to like the students? Do the students like them? Visit the cafeteria. Attend a church service. Look for a wholesome, happy atmosphere that maintains the standards of the church in a spirit of love. Get the feel of the school. The best schools have a friendly atmosphere that you can sense immediately—a camaraderie between students and faculty.

Pay close attention to the impressions you pick up. And just as important, ask your teenagers how they feel about the place. Finally, nothing is more essential than finding the right roommate.

Expense is also a factor that must be considered. If you don't think so, just wait until the school bill arrives in your mailbox! Don't be deterred, however. Proper education is crucial to your children's future life, both here and in eternity. Certainly the spiritual benefit to our young people is worth any necessary sacrifice.

However, if your best financial efforts fall short, talk with the administrators of the school you have chosen. They can be quite creative and compassionate about finding assistance.

Not always, though. I served on the board of one academy that referred delinquent accounts to a secular collection agency. That seemed an extremely regrettable practice in the light of Paul's counsel in 1 Corinthians 6. If we have to play hardball to keep a school running, it would be better to cut back the program or even close it down than to betray the spirit of Christianity.

Certainly the spiritual benefit of our young people is worth any necessary sacrifice—as long as our churches don't sacrifice the conference evangelism budget. Some well-meaning educators would siphon off soul-winning funds, saying that the most important evangelism is what we do for our own children. That sounds good, but educating our children is *nurture*, not *outreach*. Let's do one and not leave the other undone.

We have an explicit command from Christ to reach out with the gospel message to a lost and dying world. Even from a financial standpoint, evangelism is money well spent, bringing into the church tithe-paying families with additional children to populate our schools. Rather than cutting back on soul-winning, let's look for ways to spend more efficiently the mountain of money we already invest in education. We are definitely overbuilt. No doubt many of our academies and colleges ought to be consolidated—millions of dollars could be saved at no sacrifice of quality and no great inconvenience in this age of easy travel.

We could turn excess capacity into cash to invest in an endowment fund for underwriting tuition. I am told that the Adventist Church quite possibly has sufficient assets in expendable property to provide education at a tremendous discount to all our academy and college young people. Maybe even tuition-free education. Wouldn't that be wonderful!

There's a problem though—and it's quite understandable: no conference wants to lose its academy through a merger; no union conference wants to see its college close down. Part of this reluctance is an emotional tie to the past. Much of it is the simple desire to educate one's own youth rather than farm them out someplace else. But a lot of foot-dragging is just human selfishness. For whatever reasons, we want to cling blindly to what we have, despite the ever-escalating costs.

It might be asking too much to expect a local conference or union to volunteer the merger of their academy or college with another school. One possible solution might be to empower a special union constituency committee to assume control of all academies in the region. Colleges would go under the auspices of the division. Mergers would be voted as deemed necessary for the common good of all.

Would such a plan work? It wouldn't be easy. Special interest groups would no doubt be playing political hardball. Success would require untold humility, unselfishness, and mutual trust—none of which comes easy for the sinful human heart. But the day will come, sooner or later, when we'll *have to* get together so our educational system can survive. Better to pool resources than to lose them all, wouldn't you say?

Let's remember this—Adventist education calls for commitment to our youth, not to buildings and property. People are more important than the institutions themselves.

An alternate way of funding education is providing better-paying jobs for students. Harris Pine Mills for many years had been a major nationwide employer at our schools. Church leaders should counsel with competent, successful Adventist business people about establishing new industries that could be profitable for both students and institutions.

Well, for whatever it's worth, there you have my personal assessment of the Adventist educational system. If you didn't like everything you read in this chapter, I'm truly sorry. Please understand, though—to have any credibility in writing a book like this, I must be frank as well as fair.

Let me conclude with a delightful experience I had at a conference-operated campground during the autumn of 1990. I was speaking at a family-life retreat when some students from the nearby academy came to help with Sabbath School. They sang contemporary Scripture choruses and informally shared their testimonies, quoting Bible texts that had helped them in their faith experience the previous week. Let me tell you, I was impressed with those exuberant, attractive teenagers and their well-marked Bibles. They were not ashamed to talk about their best friend Jesus, whom they had come to know so well at their academy.

Wouldn't it be wonderful if all our schools provided such an atmosphere? And why not?

Some Adventists, distressed at the high cost and apparently low standards in some conference-sponsored schools, have established their own private, self-supporting institutions. From personal experience, I would express grave caution about going the independent route. Turn the page, and I'll explain why.

1. Victor S. Griffith, "Adventist Education Encompasses the World," *Ministry* (June 1990): 4.
2. George H. Akers, "The Mission of Adventist Education," *Ministry* (June 1990): 7.
3. Ibid.
4. Ibid., 8.
5. J. David Newman, "Confused Over the Basis of Salvation," *Ministry* (July 1991): 4.
6. V. Bailey Gillespie, "Nurturing Our Next Generation, *Adventist Review* (3 January 1991), 11.
7. Ibid.
8. Ibid., 7.
9. Ibid., 5.

Chapter 2

Blessing or Curse?

(Independent Ministries)

It was the autumn of 1971. I had just begun my junior year at Columbia Union College outside Washington, D.C. A fulfilling devotional hour every morning met my spiritual needs. Lots of friends and Christian fellowship met my social needs. A New Jersey state scholarship and a good job met my financial needs. The Pennsylvania Conference leaders planned to hire me as a pastor upon graduation. They suggested I begin a serious search for a life partner. With plenty of nice candidates available, I was happy to follow that counsel.

My future seemed promising. Life was wonderful.

Suddenly, everything went down the drain. I plunged into a deep, dark pit that nearly ruined my life. Just in time, the mercy of God rescued my body, mind, and soul.

It all began the evening of October 22. I was attending a student retreat in the mountains of western Maryland, hoping to enhance my joy in the Lord and my service for Christ. The speaker that weekend was an elderly minister who headed an independent, "self-supporting" institution.

There are scores of such independent ministries operated by lay members of the Seventh-day Adventist Church. They have a range of function spanning from educational institutions to media ministries and vegetarian restaurants. Most of them are eager to work in cooperation with the organized church, often under the umbrella of Adventist Laymen's Services and Industries (ASI). Many offer essential services that are impractical or even impossible for conferences to provide.

A self-supporting organization worthy of being called a ministry will not cloister itself from the church. Although financially independent, it is interdependent with the goals and purposes of the Adventist Church. It fosters denominational unity.

Unfortunately, some self-supporting organizations seem determined to wage war with the church, taking advantage of every crisis to destroy confidence in our leadership. How easy it is to criticize those who are doing their best—and doing it quite well, when you consider the multidimensional problems that our leaders must wrestle with. Here at General Conference headquarters, I'm beginning to get a grasp of what's involved in conducting the business of a world church. I can tell you this much so far—you can rest assured that the Lord is alive and at work within your church.

It would be difficult to exaggerate the damage done by certain independent "ministries," which are actually hotbeds of fundamentalist terrorism. These parasite groups siphon off funds that should go into conference projects, and a few brazenly solicit the sacred tithe. They promote themselves as being mission-oriented, but in reality they seem more interested in winning converts to themselves from among sincere but vulnerable church members than they do in winning converts to Christ.

These subversive groups might have a few highly publicized, low-cost "mission projects" to attract funding. For example, they might join the current stampede to Moscow, spend a week or two there, and come home to trumpet their accomplishments. Then they might skip over to Africa or the South Pacific to do the same thing. The goal of all this seems to be winning support for themselves that really belongs to the church body. Others, in their attacks upon church leadership, have adopted a dignified, subtle strategy that makes their legalistic deceptions all the more dangerous.

Many of the destructive independents lack any significant accountability process. One or two strong personalities control the organization, claiming divine inspiration for what amounts to egomania. They may profess to be loyal to the church body, yet they refuse to receive counsel and guidance from it.

I am particularly disturbed about attacks upon the broadcasts and telecasts of the Adventist Media Center. I worked there for eight years and became closely acquainted with all the ministries. You can rest assured that no money is being wasted; every expenditure is audited. Each speaker of the various ministries is fully committed to the Adventist message and mission. I've knelt and prayed many times with all of them. Their broadcasts and telecasts are worthy of your fervent support, without which they could not do the work God has called them to do.

So I urge you to support the work of the church God has ordained. Keep your tithes and offerings where they belong. Don't feed the wolves that are preying upon the flock.

Having said all that, let me emphasize that many independent ministries are worthy of your offerings. If you have questions about any particular group, discuss them with your pastor or conference leaders.

Now, back to my own experience with a self-supporting ministry. The particular organization represented at the student retreat I was attending sponsored a number of satellite institutions spread across North America and overseas. Its leader frequently spoke at camp meetings and other church gatherings. His organization had a well-earned reputation for cooperating with the church and its various programs, never accepting tithe funds from supporters. In fact, members of this organization faithfully returned their own tithe to the conference treasury.

Despite the basic integrity of the organization, I found some serious problems in my association with it, none of which were apparent that first night of the retreat. The only thing that struck me was the sincerity of the speaker as he solemnly began his sermon about the delay of Christ's second coming.

"Think of all the years that have passed since we expected Jesus to return," he said as his earnest eyes swept the attentive young faces of his audience. "Why has our Lord not yet come?

"The answer," he asserted, "is that Christ is waiting for every one of His people to live perfectly without sinning. We must overcome every sin before He can take us to heaven."

No, he wasn't referring to the sins of rebellion committed by the unconverted. His point was that the failure of genuine Christians to become perfectly sinless was preventing Christ from coming. He compared Jesus in heaven to a mother mopping the kitchen floor. She can't put down the mop until all her children quit tracking in mud. Likewise, Jesus can't stop what He is doing in heaven and return to earth until every Christian quits muddying up heaven's book of record by having sins to confess.

"Is this really true?" I wondered. I could feel the heartbeat of my life, the assurance of salvation, evaporating in the cool mountain air. I winced as the speaker disclosed more bad news. He informed us that every time we fail in our attempts to please God we not only delay Christ's coming but we bring crucifying pain to His loving heart. Jesus is like a railroad engineer pinned beneath the wreck of this world's sin, and our mistakes are like scalding water from a ruptured locomotive boiler dripping down upon Him. Not till every believer achieves total Christlikeness of character will the load be lifted and Christ's terrible agony cease.

"How awful!" I thought as my heart sank further. "But if it's true, I've got to accept it. How can I overcome all my sins so Jesus can stop hurting and I will be safe to save for heaven?"

"The solution to the sin problem," declared the speaker, "is to continually contemplate the terrible cost of our sins, which are breaking Christ's heart. Only then can we benefit from Christ's life-changing sacrifice. Only then will we love Jesus enough to stop sinning forever. Finally Jesus can return for His perfected people."

All this commended itself to my sensitive conscience. Not till years later did I learn that it's not the continual burden of our guilt but the peace of God, the assurance of His acceptance, that keeps our hearts and minds in Christ Jesus. "The joy of the Lord is your strength" in overcoming temptation (Nehemiah 8:10, RSV).

Yes, it's true that stubborn resistance to repentance can only be melted by the love of God that paid the cost at Calvary. But after we *do* surrender to Jesus, it's time to dispense with guilt and bask in the sunshine of His acceptance. Christians who continually brood over the awfulness of their sins tend to become psychologically unhealthy and spiritually paralyzed.

That night at the student retreat my horrified mind couldn't find rest. I tossed and turned at the agony of my Lord in the sanctuary suffering every time I missed an opportunity to witness for Him. I could hardly imagine that since my conversion, when heaven's sanctuary began processing my confessed sins, I had been torturing Jesus by my failures and delaying His coming as well.

By the time morning dawned I vowed that by faith in Christ I would overcome all sin and put a stop to His suffering. I would develop the closest possible relationship with Jesus so He could perfectly live His life in me. Then I would be ready for Him to take me home to heaven.

When I returned to the college campus after the retreat, my friends immediately noticed the change in my life. They started asking, "What's wrong, Marty? You seem depressed." (I was, although I dared not admit it.) I solemnly asked them to pray that God would help me overcome all sin and lead others to experience that vital transformation.

By Friday afternoon I had xeroxed hundreds of copies of a yellow sheet entitled "How to Stop Sinning." It was crammed full of what I had learned at the retreat. I circulated that miserable paper all over campus—in the cafeteria, the dormitories, the gym, the chapel, everywhere. I confess that I felt like a hypocrite telling everybody else how to stop sinning when I had not achieved that lofty goal.

Not because I wasn't trying, though! I rose earlier than ever to deepen my relationship with Christ and have His overcoming strength. But I encountered a big problem. The closer I came to Jesus, the more aware I was of my shortcomings—and thus the more guilty and despairing I felt.

"This is ridiculous," I thought. "Getting close to Jesus only makes me feel more sinful by comparison to Him. What will it take to become exactly like Him so I can finally have peace?"

Nothing quenched my quest for an absolutely Christlike character. Determined to quell all competitive pride, I quit playing sports. To shut down any potential temptation I refrained from dating. (Goodbye, life partner.) To keep my mind absolutely clear I stopped eating desserts. To avoid the danger of disease I gave up dairy products. In all these things I was following the rigorous blueprint advocated by that speaker from the self-supporting institution.

Do you see what was happening? A year earlier, when I became a Christian, I relinquished sin's dead leaves, but now I was breaking off life's innocent branches. All I had left was a dying stump.

What next? There wasn't a thing left to surrender that God didn't already have. All I could think of was to abandon the Christian college that permitted its students the freedom to participate in competitive sports and indulge in dating. So goodbye to all my friends. So long to my hard-earned scholarships and my cherished dream of becoming a pastor.

But where should I go? My life now revolved around the principles promoted by that self-supporting institution. I decided to make a pilgrimage there and get acquainted with the people. Perhaps they would let me join them in pursuing a perfect character.

I still remember the long journey. Every mile that passed increased my eagerness to see the New Jerusalem of my convictions. At last I drove up the winding driveway.

Paradise restored! That's what it seemed like. Simple, practical buildings way out in the country, far removed from the sinful city. Clear-eyed, smiling people with firm handshakes welcoming me to lunch. Plain, hearty food deliciously prepared. Wholesome, earnest conversation. A vigorous afternoon hike on the wooded mountain trail.

"This is the place for me," I concluded. "No foolishness. No worldliness. No compromises. These people really mean business about the straight testimony of spiritual standards."

To an earnest young Christian weary of the world's allurements, this self-supporting institution seemed to be the gateway to heaven. It appeared to be the paragon of primitive, practical godliness. Certainly, many people there were among the most sincere I have ever known. Unfortunately, I did not immediately recognize that some of them were also the most guilt-ridden, legalistic people you could ever meet.

But before I get into that, I'd like to turn for just a moment to what I see as positive.

First, I believe, as I've already said, that many of these self-supporting organizations have an important role in God's work. Our conferences simply cannot sponsor and oversee all the work Adventists ought to be doing in this vast world, especially in the areas of health-based evangelism, such as vegetarian restaurants. Independent ministries are usually practical, efficient operations that yield maximum returns from minimum resources. Employees are willing to work for wages far below what they deserve; often they work without any paycheck at all. They display a commitment that deserves our heartfelt admiration.

Furthermore, I can't think of one Adventist self-supporting organization that has a problem with worldliness. In this age of rampant compromise, we must respect such resolute fidelity to the standards of God's law and the counsels of Ellen White.

Certain church-sponsored colleges in the Adventist fellowship seem, in my opinion, to suffer seriously from secularism. Some teachers seem reluctant to give more than lip service to the fundamental and distinctive doctrines of historic Adventism. Not so in the independent institutions.

There is no question in my mind that many Adventists today have lost appreciation for our unique heritage. At the 1991 Annual Council in Perth, Australia, the General Conference reaffirmed support for the grand old pillars of Adventist faith in the "Perth Declaration." All of us would do well to read carefully that soul-searching document. This is no time to be compromising our commitment.

The independent institutions have never been afraid to stand up for Christian standards and holy living. For that, they deserve our appreciation. More could be said in favor of self-supporting ministries. A number of them admirably fulfill their God-appointed roles.

But having said that, I must share general concerns, based on my personal experiences and also conversations with scores of Adventists who have present or past acquaintance with these institutions. Keep in mind that each place has its own personality, its own combination of strengths and weaknesses.

First, many independent institutions allow their workers only limited personal freedom. At one of these places, where a friend of mine attended, two meals a day was the unwritten rule. If she wanted to munch an apple for supper, her "homeheads" forced her to eat in the cellar. Can you imagine an adult in her twenties becoming an outcast over a few bites of fruit?

When this friend requested a work assignment in the area of her preference, they deliberately assigned her elsewhere. The goal was character education, they explained—actually, the breaking of her will. Women could not wear slacks unless they also wore long dresses nearly down to their ankles. And of course the dresses had to have long sleeves.

The leaders in that institution did not trust single men and women to spend time in each other's company without someone present to monitor behavior. Single adults in their twenties and thirties couldn't even drive to church together on a sunny Sabbath morning!

The independent institution I'm describing sponsored a now-defunct missionary academy in the remote mountains of Appalachia. I was assigned there as a teacher. Things went fine until I had the misfortune of falling in love with a fellow worker.

To go about the business of romance, such as it was, I needed approval to initiate a chaperoned "courtship" (the nineteenth-century term used for dating). A man had to first get permission from the institution's leaders, and then from the woman's parents (if they were still alive). Ideally, the man would ask the leaders of the institution to suggest a wife for him. If he already had someone in mind, they usually withheld or delayed approval. Absolute authority lay in the hands of the institution's leadership. Questioning their wisdom was regarded as rebellion against God.

Social policy may vary somewhat from place to place among these institutions. I'm relating what happened to me and also a number of other people I have interviewed.

The leaders of our institution refused me the privilege of having a courtship. One major reason was my financial situation—I was too poor to consider marriage. But what chance did I have of improving my condition when they paid me only $20 a month? Especially since they forbade workers to earn outside income—and to leave the institution for any reason other than to start another institution was akin to abandoning the Lord. So how could I *ever* have the finances to get married?

Not everyone at the institution was as poor as I was. Even though we all received the same monthly allowance, both of the leaders had been wage earners in the outside world before joining the institution. They already had their furniture, a late-model car, and some money in the bank. I came to the institution with nothing but my Ellen White books and an old car bound for the junkyard. Was it fair for the institution's leaders to sit in judgment on my finances under such unjust circumstances? Nevertheless, I obediently submitted to their orders.

What perplexed me most about having my courtship denied was the directive that I "obey counsel." Obey counsel? Only a command can be obeyed—counsel is just advice. Counsel should leave me free to weigh the pros and cons and make my own decision.

I determined to get some genuine counsel from conference leaders I knew outside the system of independent institutions. When I mentioned this to the self-supporting leaders, they declared that all such counsel was invalid. They asserted that nobody but self-supporting workers really understood the straight testimony.

At this point I found myself questioning the wisdom and methods of the institution's leaders. They meant well, I assume, but who set them up as counselors above God's ordained church leaders? Where did they get the authority to control the personal lives of adults nearly their own age?

It was about this time that the conference president called me to work as a part-time literature evangelist and pastor. I had mixed emotions about leaving the institution, but there was no doubt God was calling me away. Leaving that institution was the best decision I've ever made, next to accepting Christ as my Saviour and marrying the woman they tried to withhold from me. Seventeen years later we are happily married, thankful that the Lord led us to each other.

I'm only sharing this testimony so that others can avoid

similar bondage. If you are interested in the full story of what happened, you can read it in the book *My Tortured Conscience*, available from Adventist Book Centers.

Visitors at some self-supporting institutions often find themselves impressed by what appears to be an atmosphere of happy harmony. Everybody seems so cheerfully dedicated! Only too late, after they have joined the organization, do they come to realize that what appeared to be blessed unity is really enforced uniformity.

The Bible says that "where the Spirit of the Lord is, there is liberty" (2 Corinthians 3:17). Yes, personal liberty can be abused. Even so, people need freedom to choose their own course. Isn't that one of the basic issues of the great controversy?

Ironically, many leaders who impose themselves on their subjects don't seem to feel much need of counsel themselves from those ordained by God to lead the Seventh-day Adventist Church. They chart their own course, quite indifferent to the way the Lord is leading the official church. Although they welcome the goodwill of conference presidents and want to cooperate whenever possible, there seems to be a fundamental distrust of the organized church's standards and practices.

No conference elementary school or academy anywhere seems good enough for the children of most self-supporters. As for our colleges, one of their assistant leaders told me that our academic degree program was of the devil. He said that back in the 1930s the Adventist educational system had drifted away from God and was now hopelessly adulterated by the world's standards of accreditation. He didn't understand that such a step was absolutely necessary to keep pace with the upgraded academic standards our society requires for licensing professionals. (George Knight, in his eye-opening book *Myths in Adventism*, available at Adventist Book Centers, explains the history of accreditation in our school system, along with other issues raised by critics of the church's standards.)

The truth is that, with few exceptions, independent institutions are incapable of fitting students for service in the 1990s. Nearly all of them suffer from a critically deficient academic agenda. For example, many of these places take pride in their medical-missionary training. While they do teach natural remedies that my wife and I still find useful in our own family, we had better be careful about practicing hydrotherapy on our neighbors. People are sued a lot these days. Laws have changed since the nineteenth century. Our society now has strict standards regulating medical practice. And for good reason. I could cite several instances where well-meaning but inadequately trained self-supporters caused permanent physical damage.

Since properly accredited schools are the only ones equipped to prepare students for a legitimate license in nursing or health care, self-supporting "medical missionary" training is largely a wasted effort, a broken promise. Crippled by limited medical knowledge and the lack of a medical license, students who graduate from these schools often have nowhere to work after they finish their training.

This problem extends to other areas of academics besides medical training. The sad reality is that many graduates of independent institutions have a difficult time supporting themselves in the real world. They consider their difficult circumstances a necessary Christian sacrifice. But really, poverty isn't necessarily piety. What righteousness is there in driving a rusted lowrider? And what sin is there in making enough money to care for your family and having a surplus to sponsor evangelistic endeavors?

Actually, most of the "self-supporting" institutions themselves aren't really self-supporting. Without unceasing support from donors in the real world, many of whom are college graduates, these places would go bankrupt.

Now we must address the most serious problem of independent institutions. Nearly all the self-supporting schools I'm acquainted with suffer from suffocating legalism. Please understand. Strict obedience to the commandments of God is absolutely essential in this world of sin. A life of genuine faith always leads one to be faithful to God's law. However, let's never forget *why* we obey God—it's because we love Him and appreciate His great salvation.

Unfortunately, many self-supporting organizations seem to

miss this matter of the proper motivation. To their credit they emphasize the need for holiness, but they offer little joy in the Lord and His salvation. I'm sorry to have to say that, but I can't begin to tell you how many times refugees from these institutions have poured out their shattered hearts to me. Let me share the testimony I know best.

After leaving college and joining the self-supporting system of my choice, I expected to make rapid progress toward the sinlessness they said was required to be worthy of heaven. Nothing of the world could distract me there. No television, no radio, no newspapers, no magazines, no suppers.

Survival was something of a struggle. Mornings I hand-cranked the old John Deere tractor and plowed the fields. I helped fix the rust-encrusted vehicles we drove, sawed firewood, and built little houses for incoming families. All afternoon, the year round, I sold Christian books and magazines up and down country roads and hollows. Then every evening and all weekend I conducted Bible studies in surrounding towns.

After a year of this uncompromising sacrifice in our spiritual boot camp, I was regarded as the strictest of all the people there. I ruled my appetite with an iron will. Yet my frequent fasting did nothing to satisfy my spiritual hunger. Even worse, I had to admit to myself that I still had sin in my life. No major failures such as sexual sin—just a painful sense of generally falling short of God's ideal.

I'll explain more about this legalism in the next few chapters. Let me close here on an upbeat note. In spite of the problems I've pointed out with some self-supporting organizations, the Adventist Church needs both independent and conference institutions willing to harmonize with God's purposes. The work of the Lord will prosper when we learn to work together.

Chapter 3

My Brush
With Rome

(Righteousness by Legalism)

"You Protestants really misunderstand us Catholics! In fact, to be frank, I think you often slander us."

That's what the archbishop of Buffalo, New York, told me a few years ago. We were attending a fund-raising seminar in Los Angeles and found ourselves seated together for dinner. Although his long black robe lent him an imposing presence, his affable personality soon drew me into dialogue. Before long we were discussing interfaith relationships.

"I do wish you Protestants could realize that Catholics believe in Jesus as our Saviour," the archbishop said. "We don't try to save ourselves by good works apart from Christ. Definitely not!"

Just then, the guest speaker was introduced, interrupting our conversation. He also was a Catholic, author of the book *Cloud by Day, Fire by Night*. When the master of ceremonies remarked that it sounded like a good book about celibacy, the audience roared with laughter. Actually, the theme of the book was how to maintain a faith relationship with Jesus through the trials of life. The author had much to say about the importance of experiencing the indwelling Christ.

After the speech was over, the archbishop and I rose from our table and headed for the coat rack. Before we went our separate ways he turned to me and said with a smile, "You see, Catholics really do believe in Jesus Christ."

MORE ADVENTIST HOT POTATOES

I had to admit that what I witnessed that evening was somewhat different from what I had been taught about Catholics. I determined to get to the bottom of what the church of Rome really believes. After all, we Adventists have a prophetic mandate to complete the Protestant Reformation. How can we call people out of Babylon if we don't know exactly what we are calling them from?

Seeking accurate information right from the source, I spent several days doing research at Catholic University of America. Since then I've read many hundreds of pages in Catholic literature. I'm convinced the devil has cloaked his "mystery of lawlessness" as an ingenious deception that can confuse even sincere Seventh-day Adventists.

For the last century in our own church, righteousness by faith has been a real hot potato. Sincere and dedicated Adventists often have drastically different opinions about what constitutes legalism, the wine of Babylon. Let's set aside our presuppositions and examine Catholic publications.

First, it will be helpful to take a brief tour of their church history. We must go back to the early centuries of Christianity.

The church of Rome evolved out the great apostasy foretold in the New Testament. After the apostles died, legalism ran rampant throughout Christianity. We see this in the life and teachings of the church fathers.

Take Origen, for example, an eloquent defender of Christianity against the onslaughts of pagan Rome. Despite his zeal for Christ, Origen suffered serious confusion about the gospel. He failed to understand that through the Saviour all believers stand equally accepted in God's sight. He believed that "perfect" saints, or those nearly so, enjoy special access to God, while so-called simple believers must content themselves with lesser blessings.

As the church descended deeper into legalism, those who seemed closest to attaining perfection became objects of admiration, even veneration. Their prayers were coveted as if they had a hot line to God through their superior piety.

Of course, such teaching is absolutely alien to the gospel. All believers share the same perfect record of Jesus Christ. We are either saved or lost; there are no second-class Christians. Whatever our level of spiritual growth, we all approach God through His mercy, not on the basis of our character attainments. God has no supersaints who are more acceptable to Him than the poorest struggling believer.

Around the third century, penance was introduced for the purpose of helping people take their sins seriously. Rather than rejoicing in the freedom of sins forgiven, some repenting offenders were compelled to stand conspicuously outside the church at meeting times. All this resulted from abandoning the gospel of God's grace.

Throughout the history of God's people you see problems both with permissiveness and with legalism. Both traps are from the devil, and you can backslide either way. Have you thought about it? People who pull out of worldliness often drift across the gospel freeway into legalism. The prodigal indulging in permissiveness wasn't the only backslider in the family. His brother toiling in the fields of legalism had backslidden as well, estranged from the Father's grace.

The Christian church in Rome had backslidden from God's grace into legalism. Fasting was enforced on the seventh-day Sabbath. Monastic communities sprang up for the purpose of removing worldly distractions from those who were seeking holiness.

Early in the fifth century, legalism ascended to new heights through the example of Simon Stylites. As a youth, Stylites showed unusual religious fervor. While still a shepherd boy in his early teens, he entered a monastery and dedicated himself to imitating the example of Christ. Before long, his quest for Christlikeness led him to seek total solitude. Finally he came to spend the entire Lenten season without eating or drinking, seeking to subdue the flesh and let the Spirit rule his life.

Still not satisfied with his spiritual progress, Stylites disciplined himself to stand still for long periods of time. That accomplished nothing. Finally, in the year A.D. 423, he mounted a nine-foot pillar. His goal was to live, quite literally, above the world, safe beyond the reach of its pleasures and distractions. As Stylites imagined himself getting closer and closer to Jesus, the pillars he lived on became taller and taller. Finally, he died on top of a pillar fifty feet high, never having realized perfection.

Five stories up in the air is pretty high, but not high enough to match the spiritual accomplishments of Jesus Christ. If Stylites had understood the true gospel, he wouldn't have climbed that pillar in the first place. Instead, he would have accepted Christ's perfection as his own accomplishment.

However, the Christian church of the time esteemed Stylites as a spiritual hero. Upon his death, the cities of Antioch and Constantinople competed for the possession of his body. For six centuries ascetics known as pillar saints followed his example by living up on pillars away from the world, pursuing perfection.

In all these centuries of legalism, the church of Rome never ceased to call itself Christian. To this day it promotes a perversion of faith in Christ that we might call "legalism by faith."

Let's take a careful look at this abuse of the gospel. Here are some eye-opening quotes from the *New Catholic Encyclopedia*. The first is from volume 8 under the article "Justification." "There was, is, and can be only one true way of justification—the gratuitous [free] gift of divine forgiveness offered to man in Christ and received by him in baptismal faith."[1]

And what is faith? "The empty-handed and humble acceptance of the gratuitous gift of divine mercy, forgiveness, and life. . . . There never was a way of justification by legal works."[2]

Could this indeed be the *Catholic Encyclopedia*? Sounds rather like a book from Billy Graham. Scratching our heads, we reach for volume thirteen:

"The Christian faith proclaims the fact of man's salvation, which is accomplished by the merciful act of God's love in Christ, who, by means of His life, death, and Resurrection, delivers man from the evil of sin and reunites man in grace with God."[3]

Can Catholics really be that Christ-centered? Judge for yourself:

"This new life is indeed life in Christ, so real that Paul can say, '. . . It is now no longer I that live, but Christ lives in me.' Thus justification initiates a new life which is a sharing by the Christian in the life of Christ himself."[4]

Fine so far. Grace is free, and the believer must live in union with Jesus. But then we run into trouble:

Sinful man cannot, of himself, be pleasing to God. For that, he must receive a gift from God which transforms him interiorly, cleanses him and sanctifies him by adorning him with qualities that *render him pleasing* to his Creator. Already, then, we see grace not only as a pure gift of God, which man does not deserve and cannot obtain by himself, but as something which, once given, completely changes him, by purifying him inwardly from sin, and *rendering him good and holy*.[5]

Can you see the problem? Of course, sincere Christians surrender themselves to God in order to live a life that's "good and holy," but the fact remains that we are still unworthy. All of us fall short of God's glorious ideal, the Bible says. "For we all stumble in many things" (James 3:2). Can you look in the mirror and honestly say you are "good and holy" enough to be worthy of heaven? According to the Bible, only through the blood of Jesus can God consider us worthy.

The problem is this: Catholics teach that the cleansing of the new birth renders us acceptable to God. It's true that the new birth transforms our hearts and that through the transformed heart we develop increasingly mature and holy characters. But neither the transformed heart nor the holy character that results from it qualify us for acceptance with God.

According to our Catholic friends, the gospel is this: "I cannot save myself. By faith, however, I can receive the gift of God's transforming grace through Jesus Christ. His grace changes my heart in order to make me worthy."

Rome says that our day-by-day acceptance with God is not based upon the blood of Jesus, but upon the amount of God's grace reflected in our character development. *The focus has subtly shifted from the cross to inner holiness attained by the believer.* The problem with this should be obvious: despite the miracle of transformed lives, "all have sinned and fall short of the glory of God" (Romans 3:23).

Do you see the point? Certainly grace will change our lives. But there remains that stubborn shortfall that requires the mercy of God.

Listen as our Catholic friends try to explain how God's free gift requires some additional human merit:

> Protestants conceive man's fallen state as involving his incapacity for doing any salutary act by himself. The Catholic view agrees with this but adds that *with the help of divine grace man is able to do good, the meritorious value of his good works being rooted in grace and so [is] a gift of God's grace.*[6]

Now, of course, God helps us to do good, but there is no "meritorious value" in those good works. This is not righteousness by faith, but legalism by faith! According to the Bible, salvation is not based on how much love *we have* for God, but rather on our acceptance by faith of the love *He has* for us.

That love gave Jesus to die for us as our Saviour. We can never deserve the gift of salvation, but we can—we must—surrender our lives by faith to receive what He offers in exchange for what the world offers. Remember, faith always leads us to be faithful.

Now please come with me to fifteenth-century Europe. A century before the Reformation, it's the noontime of the papacy—the midnight of the world. Symbolizing that darkness is the medieval manual on legalism by faith, *The Imitation of Christ.* To this day that Catholic devotional classic remains tremendously popular, acclaimed by the church of Rome as "the widest-read and best-loved religious book in the world, with the exception only of the Bible."[7] Here are some compelling excerpts, written about the year 1424:

> St. Lawrence, through the love of God overcame might-
> ily the love of the world and of himself. He despised all
> that was pleasant and delectable in the world. . . . Do in
> like manner, and learn to forsake some necessary and
> some well-beloved friend for the love of God.[8]

I think it was wonderful for Lawrence to love God rather than
the world. But why did he feel he had to hate everything
pleasant, even innocent human friendships? Do we see legalism
here? An unconscious desire to become one's own saviour?

I know from personal experience what it's like to give up
cherished friends—innocent relationships—not for some wholesome purpose but rather from legalistic motives. I mentioned
that in the chapter just before this one. I guess I was like
Lawrence of old, trying to get close to God so that I would finally
be good enough to go to heaven. Legalism by faith, you see.

Yes, it was to get close to God that monks and nuns abandoned their families and friends. Their good intentions were
undermined by legalism, however. The closer their relationship
with Jesus, the less time they thought they would have to suffer
in the purifying fires of purgatory.

Here is another passage:

> My son, says our Saviour Christ, I must be the end of
> all your works, if you desire to be happy and blessed. If
> you refer all goodness to Me, from whom all goodness
> comes, then all your inward affections will be purified
> and made clean.[9]

Did you know that the medieval church believed this way
about Jesus? But remember, this is legalism by faith. Catholics
look to Jesus for strength to be purified and worthy enough to
reduce their time in purgatory. Unfortunately, they fail to trust
His blood shed on Calvary as their only worthiness.

Notice another supposed quotation from Jesus in *The Imitation of Christ*:

> Offer yourself to Me and give yourself all for God, and

your oblation [offering] will be acceptable. . . . But if you
have trust in yourself and do not freely offer yourself to
My will, your oblation is not pleasing and there will not
be between us a perfect union.[10]

A perfect union with Jesus—this was the cherished goal of
medieval monks. Their earnest obsession with perfection through
a trustful relationship with Jesus is a trademark of ancient and
modern Catholic writings.

When Luther appeared on the scene in the sixteenth century,
he thundered against Rome's legalism by faith. But first, like so
many of us, he had to learn the gospel the hard way. Upon first
entering the monastery, he determined to become holy and
therefore worthy. His pursuit of purity drove him to deprive
himself of life's comforts, even its necessities. Some nights,
kneeling on the old stone floor, he would console his conscience,
"I have done nothing wrong today." Then doubts would arise:
"Am I really pure enough to qualify as a child of God?"

Nothing he could do brought him peace. He could never be
certain of satisfying God. But finally he discovered that the
peace he was trying so hard to obtain was waiting for him at
Calvary's cross. Jesus took the punishment that we sinners
deserve so we could be freely forgiven.

Luther could hardly believe this good news. Despite his guilt
he could be counted as perfect, since Jesus, who really was holy,
suffered his penalty. He finally realized that believers, though
imperfect, can at the same time be counted righteous. God
considers sinners to be saints as soon as they trust in Jesus—
even before their lives reveal good works (which, of course, will
be forthcoming).

The conflict between Luther and Rome can be summed up in
one verse, Romans 4:5: "To him who does not work but believes
on Him who justifies the ungodly, his faith is accounted for
righteousness." So the ungodly who entrust themselves to Jesus
are justified, forgiven. Forgiveness comes not because we are
holy—not by works, Luther learned—but because we have faith
in the blood of Jesus.

All his life Luther had thought it would be unfair to reward imperfect people with eternal life. His only hope for heaven was purgatory, where his imperfections could be purged after death. But at last he learned that even the saints fall short of God's perfect ideal. Our only hope is the blood of Jesus Christ, accepted by faith.

Luther came to realize that because Christ is our substitute, every Christian is already worthy for heaven. On the cross, Jesus "qualified us to be partakers of the inheritance of the saints" (Colossians 1:12). No need for purgatory! Joy filled the German priest's heart. Finally his troubled conscience found peace, and he escaped the bondage of legalism by faith.

The Protestant Reformation took northern Europe by storm. The pope, having failed to crush the gospel by his armies alone, called for a special church council in the Italian city of Trent. Church leaders met there, on and off, for eighteen years to reaffirm and refine their beliefs.

It's interesting that this Catholic Counter-Reformation did not deny the importance of looking to Christ for life-changing strength. Notice canon number three of the Council of Trent's statement of beliefs:

> If anyone says that without the Holy Spirit's pre-venient [preceding] inspiration and without his help man can believe, hope, and love or be repentant as is required if the grace of justification is to be given to him: let him be anathema [cursed].[11]

This is true. Of course we need the Spirit's help to become repentant and find justification (forgiveness). Rome's mistake was in denying that God "justifies the ungodly," that is, He forgives imperfect sinners who trust only in the blood of Jesus.

Again and again the Council of Trent statement affirms the importance of having faith in Christ. Church leaders there even emphasized the importance of obedience to God's Ten Commandments:

> 18. If anyone says that the commandments of God are impossible to observe even for a man who is justified and in the state of grace: let him be anathema.

19. If anyone says that . . . the Ten Commandments do not pertain at all to Christians: let him be anathema.

21. If anyone says that God has given Jesus Christ to men as a redeemer in whom they are to trust, but not as a lawgiver whom they are to obey: let him be anathema.[12]

It's hard to believe but true—even as soldiers under orders from Rome were persecuting Protestants, church leaders at Trent expressed confidence that God would give them power to perfectly fulfill His commandments. Notice this:

For unless men are unfaithful to his grace, God will bring the good work to perfection, just as he began it, working both the will and the performance.[13]

Wait a minute! Catholic leaders *changed* the Ten Commandments, didn't they? Only two of them. They abolished the second commandment, which forbids images. Why? Their publications explain that the purpose in making images of the saints is to honor God's perfection in their lives. Rome may mean well, but this is an expression of legalism by faith.

Catholic leaders also dismissed the Sabbath commandment. Their catechisms today report that they began worshiping on the first day because Jesus rose from the dead on Sunday and because the Holy Spirit fell on Pentecost Sunday. So to Catholics, Sunday symbolizes the resurrection power of Jesus through His Spirit to make believers worthy.

Thank God for the resurrection power of Jesus Christ. But God doesn't change our lives to make us worthy. Remember, only through the blood of Jesus are we ever worthy. Certainly Christian growth is important. But we can't confuse what the Bible calls the "fruit" of the gospel—a changed life—with the gospel itself. The gospel is what God accomplished *for us* in the life, death, and resurrection of Christ (see 1 Corinthians 15:1-4). The fruit of the gospel, the fruit of the Spirit, is loving, joyful obedience—what Christ does *in us*. What Jesus did for us on the cross is our hope of *salvation*. What He does within us is our hope of *bringing glory to God* through our life of faithfulness.

It seems incredible, but it's true just the same. Conscientious Christians—even some Adventists—can actually find themselves competing against Christ. In their misguided zeal to equal His perfect character, they may fail to find refuge in Him as their substitute. Yes, they go to Him for strength, but they don't trust His blood as their only salvation. Because of such legalism, they never have rest.

Have you ever heard it said that you cannot be sure of forgiveness in Christ? That idea came to us courtesy of Rome: "'No one can know with the certainty of faith, which cannot admit of error, that he has obtained God's grace.'"[14] To Catholics, salvation is a tightrope on which they perform by "faith." They believe "the state of grace to be always more or less precarious."[15]

Do you see the "mystery of lawlessness" at work here? Keep that word *mystery* in mind. The devil doesn't openly attack the Ten Commandments. Instead, he ingeniously undermines God's law by obscuring rest in Christ. Only true faith in Jesus establishes the law (see Romans 3:31). Without rest in Christ, zeal to obey God's law amounts to legalism.

So the "mystery of lawlessness" undermined God's law by destroying the two commandments that explicitly forbid self-righteousness. The other eight commandments they strictly obey—by God's grace, they affirm. Such is their legalism by faith.

Let me tell you about my Uncle Bill. Because he was a Catholic, I wasn't allowed as a child to visit him. That was all right with me—I was frightened of his house with all those images. I grew up and moved from New Jersey, never once having had a real conversation with him. Recently he died. Only at his funeral did I realize what a sincere person he really was. The priest described how he attended mass every morning, remaining afterward for a half-hour of personal prayer. He generously supported charities and brought encouragement to everyone who knew him. And yes, he even read his Bible. Only God will be his judge. Here's my point: I had dismissed my uncle's Catholic worship as a round of empty externals, failing to realize that every aspect of his legalism by faith had intense internal significance to him, offering some perversion of a relationship with Christ.

Why the mass? To impart the grace of Christ's sacrifice. What about the rosary? It's "a method of meditating, with the help of spoken words, on the events of the life, death and resurrection of our Lord as seen through the eyes of His Blessed Mother."[16] Is confessing to a priest a way to escape repentance? No. "Sin is an offense against God by which we lose his friendship, and we cannot expect to regain that friendship without sorrow for the offense."[17] And why penance after confession? It "provides individualized direction toward spiritual growth, eliminating evil habits, and working for perfection."[18]

Of course, Catholic legalism by faith leads them into blasphemy—the glorification of those who supposedly attained that perfect union with God. Catholics idolize Mary because through the infusion of the Holy Spirit she "is holier than all and more closely united with Christ."[19] What about venerating the other saints? "Because by honoring the saints, their relics, and images one honors God, from whom comes all holiness."[20]

You see, everything in Catholic worship involves either an attempt to be more worthy through receiving more of Jesus or the adoration of those imagined to have attained that perfect union with Jesus. All the ceremonies we Protestants find so strange are simply the logical expressions of Rome's legalism by faith.

After many years in the Adventist Church, I came to a shocking, humbling realization. Despite my aversion to Catholicism with all its ceremonies, I once basically believed its perversion of the gospel, legalism by faith. Maybe you have too. Have you ever been tempted to imagine that the blood of Christ is not good enough to get you into heaven? This deception of the antichrist has enormous appeal to the unenlightened conscience of a sincere person.

Five centuries ago the pope excommunicated the messenger of God's mercy, Martin Luther. Had he lived in the nineteenth century he might have also condemned Ellen White for this statement:

> The religious services, the prayers, the praise, the penitent confession of sin ascend from true believers as

incense to the heavenly sanctuary, but *passing through the corrupt channels of humanity, they are so defiled that unless purified by blood, they can never be of value with God*. They ascend not in spotless purity, and unless the Intercessor, who is at God's right hand, presents and purifies all by His righteousness, it is not acceptable to God. All incense from earthly tabernacles must be moist with the cleansing drops of the blood of Christ. He holds before the Father the censer of *His own merits, in which there is no taint of earthly corruption*. He gathers into this censer the prayers, the praise, and the confessions of His people, and with these He puts His own spotless righteousness. Then, perfumed with the merits of Christ's propitiation, the incense comes up before God wholly and entirely acceptable. Then gracious answers are returned.[21]

What a marvelous statement of inspiration! Rome venerates its saints and their works of faith. Ellen White says No, human channels are so corrupt that even our prayers need forgiveness. This concept is so astounding that we will spend much of the next chapter exploring it.

Our quest will be worthwhile. Speaking of Seventh-day Adventists, Ellen White declared:

There is *not one in one hundred who understands* for himself the Bible truth on this subject [justification by faith] that is so necessary to our present and eternal welfare. *When light begins to shine forth to make clear the plan of redemption to the people, the enemy works with all diligence that the light may be shut away* from the hearts of men. If we come to the word of God with a teachable, humble spirit, the rubbish of error will be swept away, and gems of truth, long hidden from our eyes, will be discovered. . . . *The enemy of man and God is not willing that this truth should be clearly presented; for he knows that if the people receive it fully, his power will be broken.*[22]

MORE ADVENTIST HOT POTATOES

It's been many years since Martin Luther proclaimed this gospel, and another century since the ministry of Ellen White. Isn't it time that all of us in the Seventh-day Adventist Church stood up and gave a certain sound to the proclamation of God's good news?

"This gospel of the kingdom will be preached throughout the whole world, as a testimony to all nations; and then the end will come" (Matthew 24:14, RSV).

1. *New Catholic Encyclopedia* (New York: McGraw Hill, 1967), s.v. "Justification."

2. Ibid.

3. Ibid., s.v. "Soteriology."

4. P. Gregory Stephens, OSB, *The Life of Grace* (Washington, D.C.: Catholic University of America, 1963), p. 33.

5. Jean Daujat, *The Theology of Grace* (London: Burns & Oates, 1959), 14.

6. *Catholic Encyclopedia*, s.v. "Justification."

7. Harold C. Gardiner, Foreword to *The Imitation of Christ* by Thomas á Kempis (New York: Doubleday, 1955), 19.

8. á Kempis, *Imitation*, 87.

9. á Kempis, *Imitation*, 118.

10. á Kempis, *Imitation*, 218.

11. John F. Clarkson, et al, *The Church Teaches* (Rockford, Ill.: Tan Books & Publishers, 1973), 210.

12. Clarkson, *Church*, 244.

13. Clarkson, *Church*, 238.

14. *Catholic Encyclopedia*, s.v. "Justification."

15. Ibid.

16. Luke Connaughton, *A-Z of the Catholic Church* (Leigh-on-Sea, England: Kevin Mayhew, 1980), 170.

17. Joseph I. Malloy, *A Catechism for Inquirers* (New York: Paulist Press, 1977), 42.

18. Malloy, *Catechism*, 44.

19. Clarkson, *Church*, 210.

20. Clarkson, *Church*, 214.

21. Ellen White, *Selected Messages* (Washington, D.C.: Review & Herald, 1958), 1:344. Emphasis supplied.

22. Ellen White, *The Advent Review and Sabbath Herald*, 3 Sept. 1889, 1, 2. Emphasis supplied.

Chapter 4

Toxic Waste in the Church

(Perfectionism)

"SINNING CHRISTIANS ARE NOT SAVED!"

So screamed the sign carried by one of the many protesters holding court outside the Hoosier Dome at the 1990 General Conference Session. Late though I was to my meeting, I had to stop and talk to the bearer of bad tidings. He seemed rather burdened and disheveled; maybe I could brighten his day with some good news.

"Would you mind if I asked you a question, brother? Tell me, are you yourself living without sin?"

He stared at me and frowned, ignoring my question.

"Tell the truth," I insisted. "You're carrying around that big sign saying Christians who sin aren't saved. You must stand behind your own gospel. Are *you* living above sin?"

Still no answer. His frown grew darker. I held my peace and went my way.

Had that poor man answered my question by saying Yes, I would have showed him 1 John 1:8: "If we claim to be without sin, we deceive ourselves and the truth is not in us" (NIV). I imagine he might have responded with Matthew 5:48: "Be perfect, therefore, as your heavenly Father is perfect" (NIV).

Be perfect! This frightening imperative sends chills up the spine of many a sincere Sadventist, destroying all joy and assurance in Jesus Christ. For more than a century—especially in recent times—the debate about perfection has been yet another Adventist hot potato.

Although some take-it-easy-Jesus-loves-you members might want to deny it, the Bible does promote perfection of character. We must get comfortable with the word *perfection*, whatever it may mean to last-generation believers.

Well, what *does* it mean? Let's discover whether biblical perfection is an absolute plateau that completely equals Christ's character or whether it's a relative state of growing maturity.

To begin with, consider what your Baptist neighbors do with the text that says "the smoke of their torment ascendeth up forever and ever." They take that relative word *forever*, turn it into an absolute, and come up with eternal torment. That's exactly what some sincere Adventists do with the word *perfection*. They turn a relative word into an absolute term and end up with torment for the tender conscience.

When we understand the truth about biblical perfection, our troubled hearts find peace and rest. The New Testament gospel is delightfully different from the discouraging things taught by the legalists among us. When we examine every reference in Scripture to the words *perfect* and *perfection*, we quickly see that they do not require an absolute state of sinlessness, as though you could see me and you could see Jesus without being able to tell the difference. No, the Bible doesn't teach that at all.

Don't take my word for it. Let's go right to that controversial text, Matthew 5:48. What did Jesus really mean when He implored us to "be therefore perfect"? The key to this passage is its parallel in Luke, where the same saying of Christ in the same context is translated, "Be *merciful*, just as your Father is merciful" (Luke 6:36, NIV, emphasis supplied). Evidently Jesus intends that in this world of hatred and selfishness we shine forth His mercy to everyone, however undeserving, even as our Father in heaven beams His sun and showers His rain on all alike. Such is the perfection God expects from His people.

The Bible says we should be "forgiving one another, if any man have a quarrel against any; even as Christ forgave you, so also do ye. And above all these things put on charity [love], which is the bond of perfectness" (Colossians 3:13, 14, KJV).

There we have it again—tender, forgiving love is the essence of perfection, not some kind of flawless performance that attempts to compete with Christ's character. Jesus prayed for His disciples that "they may be made perfect in one; and that the world may know that thou hast sent me, and hast loved them, as thou hast loved me" (John 17:23, KJV). So perfection is for the world to learn about God and His love through His loving church. It is not to qualify ourselves for a trip to heaven when Jesus comes.

Here's another text that promotes unity as God's goal for His people. "In him [Christ] you too are being built together to become a dwelling in which God lives by his Spirit" (Ephesians 2:22, NIV). Christianity is a togetherness experience. Too often those obsessed with attaining perfection neglect caring relationships in their futile quest for holiness. They seem to regard themselves as holy loners heading for the kingdom. This solitary, monastic mentality totally misses the meaning of the perfection God wants us to reveal to the world.

Let's probe deeper into this. The apostle Paul said Christ died for His church "to present her to himself as a radiant church, without stain or wrinkle or any other blemish, but holy and blameless" (Ephesians 5:27, NIV).

How can a wife be a perfect partner? By maintaining a spotless picture window, by never leaving a pillow out of place? Or by being loyal, loving, and trusting? Could Sarah burn the beans and still be a perfectly good wife to Abraham? Could she overlook a spider web in the corner of the tent and still love her man just the same?

Obviously, perfection is not focused on the purging of pickles and pepper from the diet. Health reform is important, certainly, but "the kingdom of God is not a matter of eating and drinking, but of righteousness, peace and joy in the Holy Spirit" (Romans 14:17, NIV). So let's care for our bodies in appreciation for salvation, not by making them graven images of personal righteousness to compete with the cross.

"Not so fast!" someone protests. "We must beware of lowering our standards."

Well, certainly we need to raise our standards, living as we are in the crisis hour of earth's history. "Since all these things will be dissolved, what manner of persons ought you to be in holy conduct and godliness, looking for and hastening the coming of the day of God" (2 Peter 3:11, 12). Let's raise our standards higher than ever. Ellen White said:

> God's ideal for His children is higher than the highest human thought can reach. The living God has given in His holy law a transcript of His character. . . . The ideal of Christian character is Christlikeness. There is opened up before us a path of continual advancement. We have an object to reach, a standard to gain which includes everything good and pure and noble and elevated (Manuscript 16, 1896).

We should strive for continual progress toward the goal of a Christlike character. Unfortunately, all of us have a problem, since this ideal of absolute Christlikeness is "higher than the highest human thought can reach." How often we fall short of doing even the good we know—and God's towering standard is far beyond what our conscience can possibly comprehend! No wonder the finest human righteousness amounts to nothing but toxic waste. Do you remember the quotation from the close of the last chapter, saying that all obedience is polluted, that even our prayers and our praise are defiled with selfishness?

Let me share a personal experience to illustrate how even our finest service for God is tainted by our sinfulness. One night I was flying from New York to Los Angeles, enjoying the comforts of a free upgrade to the first-class cabin, and I noticed that a young man two seats to the right of me was a recipient of many requests for autographs. "Who could that be?" I wondered. The answer came when a couple of giggling flight attendants presented him with a chocolate-covered strawberry.

"Of course," I finally realized. "That's Darryl Strawberry, the baseball player."

I have a standing agreement with my son that I try to get the autograph of any sports star I come across in my travels. So I made my way over to Darryl and got his attention. He dutifully scribbled a greeting to Steve and handed it to me.

TOXIC WASTE IN THE CHURCH

When I returned to my seat, I felt both happy and ashamed. Yes, I got the autograph, but I had missed an opportunity to say a word for Christ. It was common knowledge at the time that Darryl was going through difficult personal struggles. He needed a word of hope from God, and it was my responsibility to give it to him. Resolving to go back to him, I prayed for wisdom to know what to say.

I slowly circled around the aisle again and knelt beside the all-star ballplayer. "Darryl, there's something I always wanted to tell you if I met you."

"What is it?" he gruffly replied, understandably impatient at yet another interruption.

I looked him directly in the eye. "Darryl, when you hit a home run, the crowd cheers. When you strike out a few times, though, they turn on you. But God's not like that. Whether you hit a home run or strike out, He loves you just the same. He's got a special plan for your life, if you want to learn about it."

That got Darryl's attention. I could see he was thinking. Taking a deep breath, I ventured further, "Look, if you want, I can send you my book *Hurt, Healing and Happy Again*. It's the book my church has for special sharing this year, and I've included many stories of how God does wonderful things in people's lives.

"I'd enjoy reading that." He smiled. "Would you send it to me?"

He scribbled down his address and handed me a white scrap of paper.

Later, after the plane landed, he put on his fur coat and looked over toward me. "Will you really send me your book?"

"I certainly will," I assured him. "But is that address you gave me going to get the book to you, or will it get lost with all your fan mail?"

"Oh, no," he replied. "I gave you the address of my home. Nobody touches the mail there but me."

With that, we parted. The next morning I mailed him my book. Two weeks later I sent several gospel music tapes. A couple of weeks later I mailed a Bible. Two weeks after that I sent a compilation of scriptural promises.

I never heard anything back from Darryl. Finally I stopped

praying and sending things.

Imagine my surprise a few months later when I picked up the *Los Angeles Times* and read that Darryl Strawberry had experienced a conversion to Christ. His life had changed so completely that former teammates hardly recognized him.

I wondered, "Is it possible . . ."

Then my mother called from Maryland, all excited. A friend had seen a television interview in which Strawberry told the story of how he found Jesus. He said it all began one night on an airplane when a minister spoke to him.

"Could it really be!" I wondered. "Praise the Lord!"

Strawberry hasn't become an Adventist; he's an enthusiastic Charismatic Christian. He does tithe to his church that five-million-dollar salary, however. Nobody disputes the sincerity of his conversion.

I must confess that I haven't been shy about telling the story of Darryl Strawberry—and not just for the glory of God, I reluctantly admit. I've become quite creative in reporting my evangelistic breakthrough in ways that would make me seem humble on top of being courageous. My fine act of witnessing was polluted first by sinful fear—I almost didn't speak to Darryl at all about Jesus. After I finally did overcome my reluctance, I'm disgusted that pride pollutes every remembrance of it.

You know what I'm talking about, don't you? We can be quite clever in tooting our own horn. On the surface we apparently give all the glory to the Lord, but in reality we also promote ourselves. "Under the blessing of God," we quietly admit with unbridled humility, "for the twentieth year He helped me achieve my Ingathering goal. Praise the Lord!"

Yes, praise the Lord—but praise me a little bit too! That seems to be our attitude whenever God manages somehow to make us useful in His kingdom.

Immature children are more honest than we are—at least they don't try to hide their pride: "Me and Joe can hit the ball more far than anybody else!" We adults are somewhat more sophisticated than saying "me and Joe" in calling attention to ourselves. Our polished veneer of pride may fool people, but not God. Since even our evangelistic endeavors are polluted, no wonder that:

TOXIC WASTE IN THE CHURCH

Perfection through our own good works we can never attain. The soul who sees Jesus by faith repudiates his own righteousness. He sees himself as incomplete, his repentance insufficient, his strongest faith but feebleness, his most costly sacrifice as meager, and he sinks in humility at the foot of the cross. But a voice speaks to him from the oracles of God's Word. In amazement he hears the message, "Ye are complete in him" (Col. 2:10). Now all is at rest in his soul. No longer must he strive to find some worthiness in himself, some meritorious deed by which to gain the favor of God (*Signs of the Times*, 4 July 1892).

This compelling quotation leaves us with some heart-searching questions. We may have repented of our sins, but have we also repudiated our righteousness? Do we see our repentance as incomplete, our strongest faith as feebleness, our most costly sacrifice as meager?

What a humbling thought—our sinfulness defiles even whatever *good* things we manage to do for God. And what about all the *additional* things we ought to be doing, our sins of omission?

Here is a startling warning from the law of God: "For as many as are of the works of the law are under the curse; for it is written, 'Cursed is everyone who does not continue in all things which are written in the book of the law, to do them'" (Galatians 3:10).

The law of God demands absolute perfection—more than we have to offer. *All* things in the book of the law must be performed on a continuous basis, every waking moment, seven days a week. And this requires more than merely resisting the temptation to do something wrong or think forbidden thoughts. Remember, the law curses not just sins of commission (the bad things we do) but also sins of omission (the good things we don't do enough of).

Here we have a stunning blow to our personal righteousness. Since the law requires not just the absence of sin but perfect performance of all duty, *we might never yield to sin yet still be under the curse of the law*! Think of it!

That came as absolutely shocking news to me the first time I heard it.

MORE ADVENTIST HOT POTATOES

Then what hope do we have? I wondered. I kept reading in Galatians 3 and discovered my salvation: "Christ redeemed us from the curse of the law by becoming a curse for us, for it is written, 'Cursed is everyone who is hung on a tree'" (verse 13, NIV).

People who suffer from legalism need to understand this curse of the law, how it condemns every trace of unrighteousness as sin. Only then will they give up on attaining their own righteousness. Ironically, *the basic problem legalists have is that they don't take the law seriously enough.* They regard Mount Sinai as if it were an anthill easily conquered by minimizing the high and holy demands of God's law.

One local church elder testified, "I've been a loyal member, a faithful tithepayer, a faithful husband. I've never compromised on the standards. Through the power of Christ I believe that my life fulfills the requirements of the law."

This well-meaning man was actually blaspheming the law of God by belittling its holy requirements. He also blasphemed the cross of Jesus Christ with his self-righteousness. Certainly the characters of faithful Christians are drawn toward harmony with the law. But does that mean we can approach God without the blood of Christ, on the basis of how well we are fulfilling that law? Not unless we want a curse on our heads.

Let's be honest. As much time as we may spend in prayer, we really don't pray enough for lost souls. Do we? We don't witness enough, either. Nor have we learned all the lessons from God's Word that we should be learning. Despite our willingness to please God, our obedience is woefully inadequate, totally insufficient.

Consider the proud Pharisee in the temple, the one who thanked God he wasn't like the sinful publican. Jesus said the character attainments of that religious zealot just weren't good enough—he was under the curse of the law. But the despised publican, despite his spiritual struggles, staked his claim on the mercy of God, and Jesus said he went home justified, innocent before God.

The hope of that poor publican is our only hope too. "There is none righteous, no, not one." "There is no difference; for all have sinned and fall short of the glory of God" (Romans 3:10, 22, 23).

60

Do you see it? There is no distinction among us in terms of our personal righteousness. We all fall short of God's ideal of character perfection and therefore deserve His wrath. You and I must confess the uncomfortable fact that we're really no more worthy than the most desperate criminal cringing on death row. When you hold up my life, or your life, or anyone's life, comparing it to Christ's character, we all come up short. None of us has the least basis for boasting. "Now we know that whatever the law says, it says to those who are under the law, that every mouth may be stopped, and all the world may become guilty before God" (Romans 3:19).

What a terrifying thought—guilty before God! Life's basic problem is not that we may need a larger house or a new job or more friends. It's not even our need of a better self-image. Our basic problem is guilt before God. This is more than the mere feeling of guilt. It's the reality of our condemnation before heaven's holy law. All the earth, you and I included, stand guilty before God. Bad news indeed!

> But now the righteousness of God apart from the law is revealed, being witnessed by the Law and the Prophets, even the righteousness of God which is through faith in Jesus Christ to all and on all who believe . . . being justified freely by His grace through the redemption that is in Christ Jesus (Romans 3:21, 22, 24).

Praise the Lord, Christ's sacrifice on the cross enables Him to accept us and adopt us into His family. When we exchange what the world offers for what He offers us in Christ, we stand clean before the law—just as if we'd never done anything wrong. Even more, just as if we'd always done everything the law demands.

This is such good news it's truly hard to grasp. When I accept Jesus as my Saviour, God considers me every bit as righteous as He is. And when you accept Jesus, you are counted just that perfect too. As Christians we all share Christ's perfection; there is no difference now. When God looks at us, He smiles and says, "These are my beloved children, in whom I am well pleased." Not because of our great love for Him but because of His great love for us.

Let me say it again—the character of every sincere believer is drawn toward harmony with God's law. But victory over sin never becomes the measure of our salvation.

Remember Abraham's miracle child Isaac? As the young fellow matured and bore children of his own, did Abraham become more worthy to be called "father of many nations"? No, from beginning to end it was God's mercy alone—not that miracle in Abraham's life—that qualified him for acceptance with God. Likewise with us. Sincere faith will bring victories over sin, but not one of these miracles ever becomes the basis of whether God can accept us. *Only through the blood of Christ are we ever worthy of heaven.*

Even the most righteous saint is not good enough to stand by himself before a holy God. Consider Zechariah and Elizabeth, the parents of John the Baptist, described thus in Scripture: "Both of them were upright in the sight of God, observing all the Lord's commandments and regulations blamelessly" (Luke 1:6, NIV).

Sounds intimidating, doesn't it? God Himself witnessed that Zechariah and Elizabeth were blamelessly righteous in their commandment keeping. Amazing! But before we build a statue in their honor, let's keep reading. A few verses later we find the pious priest struck dumb for lapsing momentarily into unbelief! Evidently he was perfectly obedient in the sense that there was no "monkey business" going on in his life, yet he still had spiritual weaknesses.

A number of God's people in Old Testament times are described as "perfect," yet we find them much in need of divine mercy. Consider Job, for example. God Himself testified that "there is none like him in the earth, a perfect and an upright man, one that feareth God, and escheweth evil" (Job 1:8, KJV).

Job was perfect? He complained a lot during his suffering. He even cursed the day he was born. About the only thing he didn't curse was his family and his God. As Job's ordeal was nearing a close, God gently rebuked His servant. Job humbled himself and said, "I despise myself and repent in dust and ashes" (Job 42:6, NIV).

If Job was worthy only of dust and ashes, in what sense was he perfect? Remember that the verse we just read said he feared (respected) God and shunned evil. In other words, Job was loyal under all circumstances in his time of trouble, thus vindicating God.

Faithful Job is a symbol of the final generation, those who will go through their own time of trouble and testing to vindicate God. This explains the experience of the 144,000, who are described as being without fault before the throne of God. Without fault in the same sense as Job—remaining loyal to God under all circumstances. No stubbornness or compromised commitment.

What about Enoch and Elijah, those other symbols of the final generation, who were translated to heaven without seeing death? The Bible doesn't say much about Enoch, except that God was pleased about the way he walked with Him—so pleased that He took the patriarch to heaven without his seeing death. Again we see how one's loyal relationship to God is the essence of biblical perfection.

As for Elijah, we do know much about him. He led that mighty revival on Mount Carmel against false worship of the sun god. Later that afternoon he prayed, and rain fell, breaking a drought of several years.

A fantastic victory indeed! Surely Elijah was worthy of translation. But wait a minute. That night after his mountaintop experience, Elijah's faith faltered. He became frightened by the wicked queen and fled for his life.

What a shame. The Lord found him cowering in self-pity and had to tenderly scold him: "What are you doing here, Elijah?"

Elijah had no excuse for his hasty retreat from his post of duty. The last major act of his life was a miserable failure. Nevertheless, God in His mercy had some good news for the unworthy prophet. He told him to go back to town and anoint a successor. Why? Because God was going to take him up to heaven!

But having failed as he did, Elijah wasn't perfect enough to go to heaven, was he? Not in an absolute sense. But relatively speaking, he was perfect. Like Job, there was no compromised commitment. Through all the ups and downs of his time of trouble, Elijah never switched sides from his basic allegiance to God. So it will be with the final generation.

After examining all the evidence, we can conclude that

genuine biblical perfection involves a mature faithfulness in resisting sin, an unreserved loyalty that holds firm during times of testing. Perfection as God intends it for us is not a fussy, self-centered obsession with every freckle on our faith and speckle on our fruit. True religion does not reek with celestial chlorine but is fragrant with Mary's ointment of appreciative devotion. It's not a flawless performance but an unreserved eagerness to glorify the Lord whose love came first and free.

Chapter 5

Did Jesus
Feel Like Sinning?

(Nature of Christ)

Many hot potatoes in the Adventist oven concern lifestyle issues, such as diet, dress, and adornment. Some potatoes have to do with doctrine. Of this latter group, nothing is hotter right now than the nature of Christ.

I realized just how controversial this matter is when I addressed it in a column written for an Adventist Media Center publication. My comments unleashed a flood of unprecedented response, much of it negative.

Equally sincere Adventists disagree passionately about the nature of Christ. It seems that both sides, in addition to standing staunchly for their particular views, are trying to get the other side in trouble—perhaps even thrown out of the church. This is sad. Although I have come to some strong convictions on this matter myself, I realize there is room in the church for those who believe either way.

Let's begin with some common ground. Everyone agrees that Jesus never yielded to temptation. In that sense, He never sinned. But was His nature pure and holy like Adam's in Eden, or did He have to resist evil urges to be selfish, lustful, and impatient?

I can understand both sides of the issue. Until a few years ago, I thought Jesus had a fallen human nature just like you and I have.

"Of course not!" you may protest. "Jesus was pure and holy." Then I would have pointed you to Hebrews 4:15, which says our

Lord was "tempted in *every* way, just as *we* are" (emphasis supplied). And Hebrews 2:16 and 17 declares, "For surely it is not angels he helps, but Abraham's descendants. For this reason he had to be made like his brothers *in every way*, in order that he might become a merciful and faithful high priest" (NIV, emphasis supplied).

I used to infer from these texts that Christ walked this earth with the same carnal cravings as fallen sinners. But then I came to realize that there are indeed certain basic and undeniable differences between Jesus and me regarding temptation. For example, by the time I became sufficiently enlightened to be a Christian, I already had committed so many sins that more than twenty years later I still get flashbacks from time to time. Do you know what I'm talking about?

You see, every time we make a choice, good or bad, an electro-chemical reaction happens inside the brain. Certain cells are stimulated to form a connection that makes it easier for you to perform that same action again and yet again. Soon you have a habit, perhaps something good like morning prayer and daily exercise. Or you might develop bad habits—anything from oversleeping to overworking, from overeating to depriving yourself, from permissive behavior to legalism.

Thank God, good habits can replace bad habits. Nevertheless, we will never erase the mental record of our bad choices. Although God forgives us and empowers us to overcome our failures, permanent damage remains—as long as we live, it will be easier for us to commit a particular sin because we have done it before.

So all of us bear within our brains the baggage of all the bad choices we've ever made. Since Jesus never made any bad choices, He never had to carry that baggage of bad habits and bad memories. His mind was not scarred by a lifetime of improper thought patterns. He never had to repent and be converted. Now that's some kind of advantage!

I used to think, "Wait a minute! If Jesus had some advantages over us, would that be fair? How could He serve as our example if He didn't share our exact situation?"

Then I realized that Christ is our example in the sense of

submission to and trust in our Father in heaven. Yet that doesn't make Him our example in absolutely everything.

Let's think this through. Jesus accepted worship—do we accept worship? He forgave sin—do we forgive sin? Jesus made atonement on the cross—do we provide atonement too?

Evidently there were some differences with Jesus, compared with us. He was Immanuel, God in the flesh. That gave Him certain advantages, for which we can be thankful. But remember, any advantage He had on this earth He used to help us, thus setting us an example. We must also use any special blessings we have to aid the disadvantaged.

So I eventually learned that Jesus wasn't exactly like us and that the differences made it possible for Him to be our Saviour. Then I wondered, "But what about the new heart Christ promised to give us? Doesn't being born again with the life of Jesus make us exactly like Him?" Definitely not, I realize now. I now understand what the new-birth experience means and what it doesn't mean.

Here's what the Bible says: Having a new heart means having a new attitude, a new purpose in life, a new direction because of our new spiritual birth. Romans 12:2 says, "Do not conform any longer to the pattern of this world, but be transformed by the renewing of your *mind*" (NIV, emphasis supplied). "Let this *mind* be in you, which was also in Christ Jesus" (Philippians 2:5, KJV, emphasis supplied). The New International Version puts it like this: "Your *attitude* should be the same as that of Christ Jesus" (emphasis supplied). You see, instead of living for ourselves, we now live to honor God as Jesus did, in appreciation for His great salvation.

Despite this new heart experience, we still suffer cravings for sin. "For the sinful nature desires what is contrary to the Spirit, and the Spirit what is contrary to the sinful nature. They are in conflict with each other, so that you do not do what you want" (Galatians 5:17, NIV). Not until Jesus comes, when mortal puts on immortality, will our corruptible flesh put on incorruption (see 1 Corinthians 15:51-54). Only then will we have holy flesh as Christ changes our vile bodies like unto His glorious body (see Philippians 3:21).

So Christians in this world must endure the same sinful cravings that unconverted people have. The difference is that we have new life from the Holy Spirit, which leads us to love God and keep His commandments. Jesus never had to be born again like we do, since He was pure and holy from Bethlehem to Calvary.

Both of my children were good babies, as I recall—among the dozen finest babies in the world back in the seventies. Despite that, they inherited their father's sinful nature, becoming fussy and stubborn now and then. Did Baby Jesus get mad like that? Of course not. He was "that Holy One" in Mary's womb, according to Luke 1:35, while the rest of us are "brought forth in iniquity," "by nature children of wrath" (Psalm 51:5; Ephesians 2:3). So Jesus from His birth onward was quite different in His human nature from you and me.

Let's delve deeper into His human nature. Romans 8:3 says He came to earth "in . . . the flesh," yet only in the "*likeness* of *sinful* flesh"—that is, a form similar (not identical) to sinful flesh. In other words, He had a body like ours, but He did not have the sinful nature we have. His nature was holy, harmless, and undefiled.

Adam, in the Garden of Eden, was created in the image, or likeness of God—a form somehow similar to God's *but not identical*. It would be blasphemy to say that our likeness to God means that we are God. And isn't it also mistaken to suggest that Christ's likeness to sinful flesh means that He actually had our sinful nature?

It was this information from Romans 8:3 that really cleared up in my mind the truth about Christ's nature. He came in the flesh, but it was only the likeness—the appearance—of sinful flesh. He didn't look the same as Adam did before the fall; He looked like one of us. But His nature was pure and holy, whereas ours needs salvation.

"All that makes sense," I used to think, "but how could Jesus be tempted in all points like we are if His nature was sinless?"

Good question. I finally found the answer from studying Christ's three wilderness temptations. They provide fascinating insight into how He really was tempted.

DID JESUS FEEL LIKE SINNING?

The first temptation involved appetite and trust; Satan tempted Jesus to abuse His natural divine power and turn stones into bread. I don't have such divine power in me naturally, as Jesus did—yet in those identical areas of appetite and trusting God my sinful nature does tempt me, you can be sure.

Christ's second temptation concerned presumption, abusing divine power by jumping off the top of the temple. I've never been tempted to jump off anything higher than a pickup truck. Yet again, on this same point of presumption my sinful nature does harass me.

The third temptation enticed Jesus to abuse His divine power by winning back the world without going to the cross. My sinful nature tempts me to escape hardship for selfish reasons—not to win the world for God.

Do you see how Christ was tempted? In each case it involved abusing His divine power—while in those same areas the temptation for us is to indulge our sinful nature. To put it another way, Christ was tempted to suppress His acquired humanity and release His natural divinity. We are tempted to suppress our acquired spiritual nature and indulge our sinful humanity.

Yes, Christ was tempted in all points as we are, but from an entirely opposite direction—He the sinless Lord born in human flesh; we His sinful believers with a spiritual new birth. And by overcoming His temptations, Jesus brings us power to overcome our own temptations.

Vital to understand, don't you think? I'm glad I finally do.

Even after this truth is established from the Bible, many Adventists seem afraid to accept it until they hear an Amen from Ellen White. Some who believe Christ had a sinful nature present quite a few Ellen White quotations that appear to back their claim. They seem to overlook compelling quotations that suggest the opposite, such as these: "He is a brother in our infirmities, but not in possessing like passions. As the sinless One, His nature recoiled from evil" (*Testimonies for the Church*, vol. 2, page 202).

And from the *Seventh-day Adventist Bible Commentary*, vol. 5, page 1128: "Be careful, exceedingly careful as to how you dwell upon the human nature of Christ. Do not set Him before the people as a man with the propensities of sin. . . . He could have fallen, but not for one moment was there in Him an evil propensity. He was assailed with temptations in the wilderness, as Adam was assailed with temptations in Eden."

We all know, of course, that temptations originally assailed Adam in his sinless nature. Evidently so with Christ. Nothing could clarify that more than this statement: "We should have no misgivings in regard to the perfect sinlessness of the human nature of Christ" (*Selected Messages*, book 1, p. 256).

As for those Ellen White statements that might be interpreted the other way, George Knight explains them convincingly in his book *From 1888 to Apostasy* (available at Adventist Book Centers). He addresses the apparent discrepancies and shows how Ellen White apparently believed in the sinless nature of Christ. I urge you to buy Knight's book and read every page. It really helped clear things up for me.

Now we are prepared to confront the bottom-line concern I have with those who believe Christ had a sinful nature. They want to make Jesus exactly like us so that we can become exactly like Him in order to be saved at the second coming. Here's what they say: "We all know that Satan's original charge was that the law of God could not be perfectly obeyed. Jesus disproved that accusation through His life of perfect victory in sinful human flesh. Satan was not impressed, since Jesus was God in the flesh. In order to completely refute the devil's charge, God must now present to the universe a final generation of believers who are completely Christlike in their characters. Only that accomplishment will fully and finally defeat the devil's accusation that human beings cannot perfectly keep the law of God."

Thousands of Adventists sincerely believe that assumption. I used to be among them, till I realized that I was making an unbiblical supposition. If you doubt that, let me ask you directly: Where in the Bible does it say that Satan's original charge was that the law *could not* be obeyed? Actually, back in Eden the serpent tempted Eve to think she *should not* remain loyal and obedient. He promised divine fulfillment if she would stray from her relationship with God: "In the day you eat of it your eyes will be opened, and you will be like God" (Genesis 3:5). So Satan's original charge was that God was withholding divine enlightenment from those who remained obedient. Loyalty and the willingness to obey were the issue—attaining character perfection was not the point at all. Remember, Adam and Eve were already sinless at the time of their temptation.

Once or twice in a ministers' meeting I've offered $1,000 to anyone who can find a Bible text saying that Satan's original charge was that human beings *cannot* perfectly keep God's commandments. If you think that text is in the Bible, find it for me, would you? It's just not there—perfectionism, along with Sunday keeping, suffers from a missing text.

Here's another problem with believing that Christ had a sinful nature: the delusion that human beings in this world of sin will attain *absolute* Christlikeness. We discussed that in our last chapter, if you recall. The bottom line of sinfulness is not what we *do* or *don't do* but in what we *are*. A rattlesnake is a poisonous reptile because of what it *is*, not because of what it *does*. It only does whatever it already is. Likewise with sinners.

The final, victorious generation will indeed vindicate God as Elijah, Job, and Enoch did—not by attaining absolute sinlessness, but by remaining loyal and faithful in the great time of trouble.

Now my final concern with the concept that Jesus had a sinful nature—it used to force me into competition with Christ. Here's what I thought: "If Jesus lived perfectly in our sinful flesh, then we must do it too if we hope to be saved at His coming."

Now I know that Christ is not our competitor but our Saviour! His accomplishments are imputed to us, credited to our account, when by faith we receive His gift of salvation.

You know, I used to be so obsessed with trying to become *like* Christ that I forgot that my goal is to be "found *in* him, not having a righteousness of my own that comes from the law, but that which is through faith in Christ" (Philippians 3:9, NIV, emphasis supplied).

You may wonder, What do we need to do to be found in Christ? We simply accept the wonderful reality of what God has already done on our behalf, exchanging what the world offers for what God offers us in Christ. We see this fact of life illustrated in the life of Levi, patriarch of Israel's tribe of priests. Did you know he got credit for something his great-grandfather Abraham did many years previously? God considered unborn Levi a tithe payer because Abraham was faithful with his tithe: "Even Levi, who receives tithes, paid tithes through Abraham, so to speak" (Hebrews 7:9).

How could this be? Verse 10 explains: "For he [Levi] was still in the loins of his father [Abraham] when Melchizedek met him."

So Levi was "in Abraham" when Abraham paid tithe, and thus he received credit for his ancestor's obedience. This illustrates essential truth about the fall and redemption of the human race—what it means for us to be "in Adam" or "in Christ."

All of us died many centuries ago, according to the Bible: "Having concluded this, that one died for all, therefore *all died*" (2 Corinthians 5:14, NASB, emphasis supplied). The whole human race died together. We died twice, in fact—first in the Garden of Eden when Adam sinned, then later at the cross with Christ.

Fascinating, wouldn't you say? Let's probe this further: "Therefore, just as through one man sin entered the world, and death through sin, and thus death spread to all men, because all sinned" (Romans 5:12).

Amazing indeed. The Bible says "all sinned" with Adam, back there in the Garden of Eden. And because of it, we all met our death 6,000 years ago.

"But that's not fair," we protest. "Why should God hold us accountable for something we never did?" Well, it wouldn't be fair if He expected us to solve Adam's problem ourselves. But He sent Jesus to reconcile this world, replacing condemnation with justification. Notice verse 18: "So then as through one transgression there resulted condemnation to all men, even so through one act of righteousness there resulted justification of life to all men" (NASB).

What happened to us at Calvary counteracts what happened to us in Eden. We were "in Adam" when he sinned and brought condemnation upon the entire human family. But thank God, we also were "in Christ" when He brought salvation to "all men."

Having learned that, I found myself confronted with another question: If these events happened to us beyond our control, what about our personal freedom of choice?

DID JESUS FEEL LIKE SINNING?

Freedom to choose is restored through the gospel. We have our choice of parents—Adam or Christ, along with our choice of history—Adam's sin or Christ's salvation. We can even choose our verdict in the judgment—Adam's condemnation or Christ's justification.

So what happened to us at Calvary more than atoned for what happened to us in Eden. Justification of life came upon "all men"—yet not everyone will be saved. Only those who "*receive* the abundance of grace and of the gift of righteousness" (Romans 5:17, NASB, emphasis supplied).

Justification and condemnation—both are historical facts already accomplished. All we can do is accept one or the other.

Thanks to Romans 5, I finally understood that my spiritual successes don't save me, nor do my spiritual failures disqualify me. I was lost 6,000 years ago in Eden and then reconciled 2,000 years ago at Calvary. *Salvation depends upon which event of my past I choose to build my life upon.* My death in Adam will doom me. My death and new life in Jesus will save me.

Reconciliation with God is an accomplished fact. "God was in Christ, reconciling the world unto himself" (2 Corinthians 5:19, KJV). The question today is not, Can I be saved, but, Do I want to accept the salvation I have already achieved in Christ?

This gospel that assures my salvation also provides wonderful possibilities for victory over sin. Not only did Jesus conquer the penalty of sin at Calvary, He also conquered its power. The question now is not, Can I be victorious, but, Do I want to accept my victory already achieved in Christ?

Unfortunately, some would-be Christians want pardon but not power. They ask, "Since 2,000 years ago I fulfilled the law in Christ, why must I live obediently today?" The Bible leaves no room for misunderstanding: "What shall we say then? Are we to continue in sin that grace might increase? May it never be! How shall we who died to sin still live in it?" (Romans 6:1, 2, NASB).

Sin's power has ended—never again need we yield to temptation: "He who has died is freed from sin." "Even so consider yourselves to be dead to sin, but alive to God in Christ Jesus" (Romans 6:7, 11, NASB).

Notice that my death to sin is not something I accomplish when I decide to repent. I died at the cross, remember? Now I simply accept my death in Christ and the resurrection victory I already won in Him back then.

Baptism is the symbol through which we accept our death and resurrection in Christ that happened 2,000 years ago. Sometimes this reality escapes us. We speak of Jesus becoming baptized as our example. But there's more—He was baptized "'to fulfill all righteousness'"(Matthew 3:15, NASB). In His life and death He fulfilled *all* righteousness on our behalf. His work counts on our behalf. We enter His rest, we accept His victory. We don't copy it—we receive it, we live it.

You know, it's one thing to understand Christ died for us, but it's quite another thing to realize we also died in Him. We died at the cross; through baptism we now signify our decision to choose Christ over Adam and participate in His victory. So victory over sin is our spiritual birthright. There is power in the gospel to keep us from falling when tempted.

Now, suppose I surrender myself sincerely to Christ but find myself frustrated in experiencing victory. What if I fall short of mastering all the possibilities of Christian living. Am I lost?

Not at all. That would make my character now compete with what I've already accomplished 2,000 years ago in Christ. Remember, just as Levi fulfilled the law "in Abraham," we fulfilled the law "in Christ." Through Him we have already "fulfilled *all* righteousness." Today we can only accept or reject that righteous record—we don't compete with it.

Satan has two great traps for the Christian, the goal of both being the same—separating ourselves from what Christ has already accomplished. First, the enemy wants us live in the flesh, indulging in Adam's failure as though we never died to the power of sin in Christ. But suppose we escape that snare of the world and yield ourselves to live for God? Then Satan tempts us to compete with our righteous record already established by the perfection of Christ's obedience.

Remember, I'm neither saved by my spiritual successes nor lost by my failures in my moments of weekness. No need to duplicate Christ's accomplishments today. His perfect record is mine.

DID JESUS FEEL LIKE SINNING?

Well, then, what is the purpose of my character development, if not to earn me a ticket to heaven? It's to glorify God! He is "able to do exceeding abundantly beyond all that we ask or think, according to the power that works within us, to Him be the glory in the church" (Ephesians 3:20, 21, NASB).

So the purpose of God's transforming power is to bring glory to His name—not to compete with something already accomplished 2,000 years ago. We accept Christ's life and death as ours, not trying to establish a separate identity in competition with His accomplishments.

Let's never confuse the possibilities of Christian living with the requirement for salvation. Christ fulfilled all righteousness for us on the cross—what must happen now is that we repent and receive His new life. Then, in the joy of that salvation, we live to glorify God in this dark world by sharing the light of His love. Such is the keeping of the commandments that blossoms from our faith in Jesus Christ.

I realize that much more could be said about commandment keeping and victorious Christian living than I could possibly have space for in this chapter. Surely the Lord has much more power available than we appropriate for daily living. I'm so glad that His mercy is always there as well. When we fail, even in His power, to fulfill our potential, His mercy never fails to cover our shortcomings—assuming, of course, that we are living in a state of sincere repentance.

Once I finally understood that, I was able to grasp the truth about the nature of Christ. I know this is a much deeper subject than I've been able to cover here. I just hope my testimony has been helpful.

More than anything else about Christ's nature, let's remember that He had a loving nature. He was even gracious to those who disagreed with His theology. Through the power of His love in us, may we be the same.

Chapter 6

Jesus Yes, Judgment No?

(1844 and the Judgment)

Have you heard of the "Last Hope of the Church Committee"? Probably not. Some friends and I formed a study group and modestly referred to ourselves by that name, all in good fun. The subjects we discussed month by month, however, were very serious. One evening we met in my living room to debate the judgment of 1844 in heaven's sanctuary.

Perhaps we had our Bibles open and our minds closed, because we didn't seem to be getting anywhere. Finally one of my friends turned to me in exasperation. "Tell me honestly, what difference does it make? I know I'm accepted in Christ, so what difference does it make whether or not there's a judgment going on in heaven right now?"

Even outside our Last Hope of the Church Committee, the 1844 judgment has become a scorching hot potato in the Adventist Church. Much is at stake, since our sanctuary message provides the doctrinal foundation of the Seventh-day Adventist Church. Other churches may teach the Sabbath and the second coming as we do. Some even believe in the spirit of prophecy (at least in theory), but nobody shares our conviction that in the year 1844 a judgment began in heaven's sanctuary. This doctrine is God's unique gift to our church. If you do away with the sanctuary and the judgment, you undermine our biblical mandate for existence. We might as well be Seventh-day Baptists.

MORE ADVENTIST HOT POTATOES

Who can deny that the devil has aimed his sharpest arrows at the sanctuary and the 1844 judgment? I find it disappointing that many Adventists are unable to defend this doctrine from the Bible alone. When confronted with honest, probing questions about 1844, they quickly drop their Bibles and resort to the writings of Ellen White.

Thank God for the prophetic gift given to our church, but let's not abuse it. If we take our prophet seriously, we will accept her admonition to make the Bible our only rule of faith and doctrine. Everything we present as testing truth must be provable from the Scriptures. Otherwise we make ourselves seem like a nonbiblical cult.

Some members, seeking to establish a biblical foundation for their faith, quietly dismiss the 1844 judgment. To them, it's Jesus yes, judgment no. They regard themselves as enlightened Adventists, liberated from legalism.

We cannot deny that legalism has been a sledgehammer Satan has been using to dismantle faith in the sanctuary. He has enjoyed a measure of success. Let me prove that by asking you a quick question: What comes to your mind when you think of the Most Holy Place, the second compartment of the sanctuary?

Automatically, many Adventists think of the law. But why, when all the action in that apartment took place at the mercy seat—that slab of gold where the blood was sprinkled? God specifically said He would meet with His people from above the mercy seat (see Exodus 25:22). Then why do some of us think only of the law in that second apartment?

Legalism, that's why.

The fact is that God cannot relate to unworthy sinners on the basis of how well we are fulfilling His law. He must meet with us at the mercy seat. After a century and a half of claiming to proclaim the truth about the sanctuary, I'd say it's about time we got that straight, don't you think? It's high time we flushed away all that legalism and preached the pure gospel truth about the sanctuary.

Some of the most depressing, faith-destroying fallacies in the history of Christianity have corrupted the minds of many Adventists through misunderstanding the sanctuary and the judgment. I remember as a child being threatened week after week in church and day after day in church school. The goal was good behavior, motivated by an incessant bombardment of guilt and fear: "Unless you become absolutely perfect in character, you cannot be saved when Jesus comes. Even now your name might have come up in judgment, and you might already be past the close of probation."

Several of my classmates were convinced that their probation was past and that they had committed the unpardonable sin. "What's the use of even trying?" they would lament. So they gave up hope and gave up God. More than twenty years later, most of them are still out of the church. Thanks to legalism. What a shame!

Other students, myself included, gritted our teeth and kept climbing those steep stairs to absolute perfection. We hoped someday to deserve being saved by grace. Unfortunately, everything we did for God was corrupted by guilt and fear, amounting to nothing but dead works. Jesus said, "If you *love* Me, keep My commandments." "There is *no fear in love*, but perfect love casts out fear, because fear involves torment. But he who fears has not been made perfect in love" (John 14:15; 1 John 4:18, emphasis supplied).

It should not surprise us that some Adventists, seeking spiritual security, have rejected the whole concept of a celestial pre-advent judgment. They wonder, "Why should we who are already 'accepted in the Beloved' have to face the scrutiny of judgment? Didn't Jesus Himself say that ' "he who hears My word, and believes in Him who sent Me has everlasting life, and shall not come into judgment" ' (John 5:24)?"

"No," protest the defenders of the faith. "Our King James Bible teaches that believers *are* judged. We escape 'condemnation,' but there is still a judgment all must face."

Then those who reject the pre-advent judgment inform us that the King James, while normally reliable, is inconsistent here. In John 5:22 the Greek noun *krisis* is correctly translated *judgment*, but two verses later the same word in the same context is changed to *condemnation*. However, even that favorite Adventist passage, Revelation 14, employs *krisis* to proclaim that 'the hour of His judgment is come' (verse 7). Not the hour of His condemnation, but of His judgment.

The late Walter Martin, who was the world's foremost authority on cults, charged that "in John 5:24 the Greek deals a devastating blow to the Seventh-day Adventist concept of Investigative Judgment."[1] Can we ignore the challenge of this evangelical Goliath?

Those who dismiss Adventist doctrine press their point with another perplexing passage: "He who believes in Him is *not* judged" (John 3:18, NASB, emphasis supplied). "This makes sense," they assert. "Why must God spend more than a century investigating records when ' "the Lord [already] knows who are His" ' (2 Timothy 2:19, NASB)?"

These questions bring considerable consternation. Sometimes we try to escape them by finding refuge in those safe and familiar passages that cement our doctrinal structure—texts such as James 2:12: "So speak and so do as those who will be judged by the law of liberty." Paul warns that "we must all appear before the judgment seat of Christ" (2 Corinthians 5:10). Those who support the traditional view assure us that "the work of Christ does not release us from accountability. We are told to 'give an account of your stewardship' (Luke 16:2). Wherever there is accountability, there is judgment. Surely these Scriptures all show that Christians must face judgment."

"Wait a minute!" another challenger intrudes. "You can't quote Paul to prove the investigative judgment. He tells us Christ is the judge. You say He's your defense attorney. How can Jesus both judge believers and represent them at the same time? You can't have it both ways."

Oh, well. Back to Revelation 14. There it clearly states that during earth's final gospel proclamation "the hour of His judgment *has* come."[2]

And so it goes. Many honest seekers of truth, thoroughly confused, wonder what to do. For a while, I found myself perplexed about these questions. I'm so happy to have them completely settled in my mind. I can testify that the gospel truth about the judgment going on in heaven's sanctuary inspires me with hope and assurance, confidence in my salvation.

JESUS YES, JUDGMENT NO?

The key to my new understanding is the ancient Hebrew meaning of judgment, which was quite different from our Western legal system. Our society requires judges and juries to be strictly neutral. If they harbor a bias either in favor or against the accused, our law demands that they disqualify themselves. Not so in Bible times. Back then, the legal code required judges to abandon neutrality and take the side of the defendant. The defense of the accused was a duty so sacred that the judge refused to delegate it to a defense attorney. Instead, he himself served as the defender of the accused.

The *Jewish Encyclopedia* explains, "Attorneys at law are unknown in Jewish law."[3] Their legal code required judges to "lean always to the side of the defendant and give him the advantage of every possible doubt."[4]

Witnesses of the crime pressed charges, while the judge promoted the case of the defendant, biased in favor of acquittal.[5] Of course, the judge also had to execute justice. If evidence of guilt could not be controverted, he had to reluctantly abandon his defense of the accused and pronounce condemnation. But the whole Old Testament system was predisposed toward vindication, not condemnation.

A wonderful concept, but it leaves us with a question: If God is defending us in the heavenly judgment, who would dare withstand Him? Actually, it's the devil who raises questions about our salvation in the judgment. The Bible calls him the "accuser of our brethren," who "accuses them before our God day and night" (Revelation 12:10). More about this later.

Now, in certain situations the Hebrew judge appointed an advocate to assist him in defending the accused. The *Jewish Encyclopedia* states that the husband could represent his wife and help the judge defend her if the verdict involved his personal rights.[6]

Here we have a thrilling parallel with the heavenly judgment. Christ, the Bridegroom of the church, purchased us with His precious blood. Now He serves as our court-appointed advocate to help the Father defend us from Satan—and to defend His own right to take us to heaven and share His home forever. Wonderful news! God in the judgment takes our side against Satan.

Jesus our advocate assists Him by interceding for us. God finds in the sacrifice of His Son the legal basis to accept repenting sinners and count us perfect. I like that, don't you? It makes me feel confident in Christ about my salvation!

Now we see how Jesus, our judge, can also serve as our defender. There is no conflict in His dual role—it is, in fact, necessary for Jesus to defend us as our judge.

Another evidence of God's love for His children is shown by a further provision of the Hebrew legal system:

> In the nature of things some parties cannot plead for themselves. Infants, boys under thirteen or girls under twelve, the deaf and dumb, and lunatics can plead only through a guardian; and it is the duty of the court to appoint a guardian for such, if they have none.[7]

We are helpless, unable to defend ourselves from the devil's accusations. So our loving Father in heaven has appointed a sympathetic high priest to intercede for His children against the vicious charges of our adversary.

Back in 1980, when I first understood this good news about the judgment and the sanctuary, the Lord gave me a special illustration. It came to me in the supermarket, of all places. I was standing in line with my wife Darlene, leaning on our grocery cart. Our children found themselves utterly fascinated by the candy rack, hoping to persuade us to let them have an unscheduled treat.

First they tried Milky Way bars. Nothing doing. Then M&M's ("These have peanuts, and peanuts are good, aren't they, Daddy?"). When that failed, they reached for the last resort, sugarless chewing gum. You parents know what I'm talking about.

Anyway, this was going on when a wonderful realization suddenly struck me. Here we were, waiting so confidently in the checkout line without any doubts that the groceries were going to be ours—this despite the fact that there was a judgment of sorts to pass before we could take the goods home.

You see, the clerk had to decide if we were "worthy" of having the groceries. And what was it that qualified us? It was the money we had in our hands. With cash to present the clerk, the groceries would unquestionably be ours to take home.

Heaven's judgment is something like that. Jesus is the treasure we need to pass the celestial checkout. With Jesus we can be assured of a favorable verdict, whatever our sincere struggles may be. God isn't threatened by our faults and failures. Just as the Safeway supermarket decided beforehand that whoever has money qualifies for groceries, God has declared that everyone who is in Christ qualifies for heaven.

Can you see it? The test of the judgment is not whether we are worthy in ourselves. Our own goodness does not come into judgment. The question is whether we have faith in Christ—we choose our verdict in the judgment by identifying ourselves with Christ's act of justification instead of Adam's act of condemnation.

You understand, I'm sure, that this is not some cheap, second-rate gospel that permits all kinds of monkey business under the guise of faith. True Bible faith requires wholehearted commitment—commitment to Christ that exchanges what the world offers for what He offers.

Well, I was thrilled with what the Lord revealed to me about the judgment as I waited in the supermarket checkout line. He gave me a much better treat than my kids were hoping to get.

But I still had the question: Why even *have* a judgment if God already knows who believers are?

Obviously, it isn't for the sake of informing God of something He doesn't know, so it must be to enlighten His creation. Here we need to consider the background of the great controversy between good and evil.

Satan, the father of all lies, long ago raised doubts about God's fairness and integrity. He repeated these charges during Christ's days on earth: "This man receiveth sinners!" In other words, "How can the Holy One accept those who are unholy? And if He can forgive sinners, why cast me and my angels out of heaven, yet build mansions there for fallen humanity?"

A number of texts show that celestial beings are intensely interested in questions concerning our salvation.[8] God can't brush aside the devil's accusations. Since His government operates through the loving trust and loyalty of the universe, He must settle doubts about His trustworthiness. The Bible reveals that God will allow Himself to be audited: "Let God be true, but every man a liar; as it is written, That thou mightest be justified in thy sayings, and mightest overcome when thou art judged" (Romans 3:4, KJV).

One more thing about the investigative judgment. Sometimes people feel bad about having their sins recorded in the sanctuary. But actually, as long as we remain in Christ, our sins are forgiven and guilt is gone! So it's not so much a record of our sins that God is keeping up there as it is a record of His forgiveness, His mercy in our lives.

There you have the biblical meaning of judgment for sincere believers. God is on our side, defending our salvation. Many Sadventists are becoming Gladventists through discovering this truth about our heavenly Father. Now they can rejoice in the reality of a celestial pre-advent judgment, but they may still have doubts about exactly when this judgment begins. Doctrinal controversies have destroyed their faith in our historic prophetic timetable.

Often someone will take me aside and say, "Tell the truth. You don't really believe this 1844 business, do you? You're just marching in place so you can keep a job that lets you do a lot of good for the gospel in the Adventist Church."

I always cringe when people talk like that. "How can anyone even think of playing political games with God's truth?" I ask them. Then I quickly give a little Bible study explaining how I've concluded that the 1844 judgment is truly biblical. I base my convictions on four simple facts. Follow me carefully:

1. *One prophetic day equals a literal year.* Adventists did not invent this principle of prophetic interpretation. It is the Protestant position held by the Reformers themselves 500 years ago. Far more effective than the proof-text method is the convincing contextual evidence for the day/year principle in the time prophecies of Scripture.[9]

2. *There is linkage between Daniel chapters 8 and 9.* Chapter 8 ends with Daniel's perplexing testimony: "I was appalled by the vision; it was beyond understanding" (Daniel 8:27, NIV). In the

next chapter an angel arrives in answer to the prophet's prayers, announcing: "'I have now come to give you insight and understanding. . . . Therefore, consider the message and understand the vision'"(Daniel 9:22, 23, NIV).

What vision was the angel referring to? The only possible answer is the vision left unresolved by the previous chapter. Thus the explanation of Daniel 9 solves the mystery of Daniel 8.

3. *The 490 years of Daniel 9 are "cut off" from the longer time span of 2,300 years.* Listen to what Desmond Ford himself wrote in his 1978 commentary on *Daniel*: "All Hebraists assert that its literal meaning is 'cut off.' The seventy weeks of years are 'cut off' from the longer period of 2300 years, and they commence with 'the going forth of the word to restore and build Jerusalem.'"[10]

4. *The starting date for the 2,300-year prophecy is 457 B.C.* Archeology has now documented the Adventist timetable for the historic decree to rebuild Jerusalem. A recent Zondervan book widely advertised and acclaimed among evangelicals, *Encyclopedia of Bible Difficulties*, also sets 457 B.C. as Daniel 9's prophetic starting date (although no connection is made with Daniel 8).[11] Actually, during the past thousand years, literally hundreds of illustrious Protestant, Catholic, and Jewish scholars have interpreted Daniel's 2,300 days as literal years, many of them placing its starting date in the fifth century B.C.[12]

Bolstered by this evidence, we can be convinced beyond question that all four of the above statements are true. That means the year 1844 is the legitimate fulfillment of Daniel 8 and 9. Bible-believing Seventh-day Adventists can rest secure in our prophetic heritage regarding the sanctuary and the judgment. We are standing on solid ground—that is, as long as we keep our gospel focus. If we lose sight of the cross, we forfeit our firm foundation.

Many Adventists really want to relate to God in the sanctuary with a heart filled with love and assurance, but they stumble over that solemn phrase, "He that overcometh," repeated in each message to Revelation's seven churches. The problem is, how do we know when we have overcome enough to be saved?

Let me ask you a simple question: "He that overcometh" *what?* Look at the context. The obvious answer is he that overcometh whatever problems or challenges are mentioned about that particular church. Regarding Laodicea, for example, the problem to overcome was lukewarmness. Do you see?

Sometimes this overcoming is not about victory we experience in overcoming sin, but rather in overcoming our accusers. Earlier in this chapter we read from Romans 3 about God overcoming when He is judged. He doesn't have any sins He needs to overcome, of course. Remember, He is overcoming in the celestial courtroom, overcoming the accusations of the devil.

In that same judgment setting we overcome those charges by Satan about our own situation. We saw in Revelation 12:10 that he accuses us day and night of being unworthy of salvation. According to the devil, any grounds for accusation in our lives, any imperfections, disqualify us for heaven. Evidently Satan's doctrine of righteousness by faith is that you have to be perfect to go to heaven. So *the devil is the original perfectionist.* Now that's something to think about!

Well, we are unworthy, aren't we? How do we counter his accusations?

Notice the next verse in Revelation 12: "They overcame him because of the blood of the Lamb and by the word of their testimony" (verse 11, NIV).

Our testimony is about Jesus Christ. We overcome in the judgment on the basis of His blood. It's only through our Saviour that we can conquer the devil's accusations. God cannot deny Satan's contention that we are sinful, but in the blood shed on Calvary's cross He finds the evidence He needs to pronounce us innocent. So He dismisses Satan's charges, endorsing the security in Christ we have enjoyed since we accepted Him.

The Bible says that the moment we repent and accept Jesus we are ready to meet Him, instantly qualified as citizens of heaven. Notice this: "Giving thanks to the Father, who has qualified us to share in the inheritance of the saints in light. For He has delivered us from the domain of darkness, and transferred us to the kingdom of His beloved Son, in whom we have redemption, the forgiveness of sins" (Colossians 1:12-14, NASB).

You may be thinking, "I really want this assurance. But how far does it go?"

Well, it certainly isn't once saved, always saved. Absolutely not! The devil himself lost his position in heaven by rebelling against God. If we choose to revert to fallen Lucifer's lifestyle, we will also get ourselves cast out of our heavenly position in Christ. But if we are willing to reaffirm our repentance day by day and keep our faith in Jesus Christ, we can rejoice in the assurance that we are already citizens of His kingdom, sitting with Him in heavenly places. And since God says we are citizens of heaven now, why should we worry about getting there when Jesus comes?

You may wonder, though, about the close of probation—where will our hope of salvation be then? Remember the Old Testament time of trouble with the plagues before the exodus to the Promised Land: "The blood shall be a sign for you . . . and when I see the blood I will pass over you" (Exodus 12:13, NASB).

The blood of Jesus! That's where our hope is—never in our character attainments. When Christ comes in the clouds and the awesome question goes forth, "Who shall be able to stand?" His comforting answer will be, "My grace is sufficient for you."

I can't begin to tell you what peace with God through the blood of Christ means to me. Now I really want Jesus to come—and the sooner the better.

---

1. Walter R. Martin, *The Kingdom of the Cults* (Minneapolis, Minn.: Bethany House, 1965), 406.

2. Note the timing of this judgment. Christ will not come until after the close of the gospel proclamation (see Matthew 24:14). Since this judgment accompanies the preaching of the gospel, it must precede the return of Jesus—a pre-advent judgment.

3. *The Jewish Encyclopedia* (New York: Funk & Wagnalls, 1904), s.v. "Attorney."

4. W. M. Chandler, *The Trial of Jesus*, 1:153, 154.

5. See Taylor Bunch, *Behold the Man!* (Nashville: Southern Publishing, 1946), 64, 66. Now we understand why David in the Psalms longed to be sentenced by divine judgment: "Judge me, O Lord my God, according to thy righteousness; and let them not rejoice over me" (Psalm 35:24, KJV). Throughout the Old Testament, God's people found joy in His judgment: "A father of the fatherless, and a judge of the widows, is God in his holy habitation" (Psalm 68:5, KJV).

6. *Jewish Encyclopedia*, s.v. "Attorney."

7. *Jewish Encyclopedia*, s.v. "Procedure in Civil Causes." The Father gave Jesus "authority to execute judgment also, because He is the Son of Man" (John 5:27). Both Father and Son work together to defend us, so *both* are considered our judge (compare Hebrews 12:23, 24 with Acts 10:40-42). Both are also called

"saviour" (Titus 1:3, 4) and "creator" (compare Mark 13:19 with John 1:3). All three members of the Godhead work concertedly.

8. Consider texts such as 1 Peter 1:12; Ephesians 3:10; 1 Corinthians 4:9; and Exodus 25:20.

9. Ironically, Desmond Ford (who perhaps has done more than anyone to destroy confidence in our prophetic heritage) himself offered quite a compelling defense of the day/year principle in his 1978 commentary on Daniel. His words are forceful and persuasive: "Inasmuch as short-lived beasts are employed as symbols of long-existent empires, it is most likely that the times mentioned are also presented to scale, with a small time unit representing a larger one" *(Daniel,* [Nashville, Tenn.: Southern Publishing Association, 1978], 302).

"The context of both Dan 7 and 8 forbids the idea that the periods mentioned could be literal. In the first case the little horn emerges from the fourth world empire and endures till the time of the judgment and the advent, and 7:25 declares that the period of 'a time, two times, and half a time' extends over most of this time. How impossible this would be if three and a half years only were intended! Similarly, in 8:17 the prophet is told that the 2300 days would extend from the restoration of the sanctuary until 'the time of the end.' This means that a period of approximately 2300 years is involved. The treading down of the sanctuary brought to view in 8:11-13 could not begin before the restoration spoken of in 9:25, in the fifth century BC. And besides this, its terminus is expressly stated as belonging to the latter days, just prior to the final proclamation of the gospel by the 'wise' (see 12:3, 4). It has been largely overlooked by critics that 8:17, when linked with 12:3, 4, 9, 10, 13, makes it conclusive that the 2300-day period covers many centuries. Likewise in Rev 12 the forty-two-month period covers the greater part of the time between the first and second advents, when the church would be in the wilderness of persecution during the Dark Ages. This is granted by almost all expositors" (ibid.).

"Are there any indications in the rest of Scripture that God has ever chosen such [day for a year] symbolism? In Num 14:34 and Eze 4:6 we find evidence that such is the case. God has chosen on other occasions to use precisely this symbolism; one of these occasions was during the time of Daniel's captivity, and its use was in connection with a contemporary prophet" (ibid.).

One wonders how Dr. Ford could abandon such scholarship and turn against our historicist prophetic heritage. William Shea adds additional weight to the case for considering a day to represent a year: "With the description of literal persons, places, and events in classical prophecy one naturallay [sic] expects literal time units to be employed. With the symbolic figures found in apocalyptic, on the other hand, one naturally expects to find symbolic time employed. This leads to the general rule—literal prophecy: literal time—symbolic prophecy: symbolic time" (William Shea, "The Year-Day Principle in Prophecy," *Pacific Union Recorder*, 22 September 1980, 2).

Shea then concludes: "The application of a day for a year in apocalyptic prophecy has been a standard principle of Protestant prophetic interpretation from the time of the Reformation in the 16th century to the 19th century. With the rise of literary criticism of the Bible in the 19th century, the critical school of interpreters abandoned this principle in favor of interpreting these apocalyptic time periods as all having been fulfilled literally in the past, during the days of the Hellenistic kingdoms and the Roman Empire. The majority of Evangelical scholars now apply some of these time prophecies in the future with literal time for a yet future antichrist. . . . At this time in our Church history when our attention has been called to some of the doctrines of the Reformers, such as justification and righteousness by faith, we would do well to heed their principles of prophetic interpretation also" (ibid.).

10. Ford, *Daniel*, 207. Here is further testimony from Desmond Ford's 1978 commentary actually confirming historic Adventist prophetic interpretation: "The pragmatic test should now be applied and the question asked: Have any of Daniel's prophecies already met with a precise fulfillment that accords with the [day/year] principle we are studying? Dan 9:24-27, the prophecy of the seventy weeks, seems to offer just such a fulfillment. . . . Inasmuch as other evidence shows that this period of 490 years is cut off from the longer period of the 2300, it is obvious that the latter must consist of years also. Thus here in Dan. 9 we have the pragmatic test met, and the year-day principle justified, despite the fact that the word *day* is nowhere used in this passage" (ibid., 302, 303).

Ford also quoted Philip Newell's commentary: " 'The Hebrew word used here . . . has the literal connotation of "cutting off" in the sense of severing from a larger portion' " (Ford, *Daniel*, 225). *The Pulpit Commentary* concurs: " 'Determined' (KJV for 'decreed', as already indicated, means 'cut off' " (*The Pulpit Commentary*, ed. H. D. M. Spence [New York: Funk & Wagnalls, 1950] 13: 218). The lexicon in *Strong's Concordance* also concurs, along with *The New Brown, Driver and Briggs Gesenius*.

11. Gleason L. Archer, *Encyclopedia of Bible Difficulties* (Grand Rapids, Mich.: Zondervan, 1982), 290.

12. Among Catholics "about 1292 Arnold of Villanova said that *the 2300 days stand for 2300 years*, counting the period from the time of Daniel to the Second Advent. . . . Better known to most church historians is the illustrious Nicholas Krebs of Cusa, Roman Catholic cardinal, scholar, philosopher, and theologian, who in 1452 declared that the 2300 year-days began in the time of Persia" (*Seventh-day Adventists Answer Questions on Doctrine* [Washington, D.C.: Review and Herald, 1957], 311).

"In the century after the Protestant Reformation, many Protestant expounders from English theologian George Downham (died 1634) to British barrister Edward King in 1798, declared the number 2300 involved the same number of years. John Tillinghast (died 1655) ended them at the second advent and the 1,000-year reign of the saints. Tillinghast was *the first to assert the 70 weeks of years to be a lesser epoch within the larger period of the 2300 years*" (ibid., 312).

John Fletcher, an associate of John Wesley, in 1755 interpreted the cleansing of the sanctuary as a restoration of truth from papal error at the end of a 2300-year period that began with Persia (see LeRoy E. Froom, *The Prophetic Faith of Our Fathers* [Washington, D.C.: Review and Herald, 1954], 2:688).

"Johann Petri (died 1792), Reformed pastor of Seckbach, Germany, in 1768 introduced the final step . . . leading to the inevitable conclusion and climax—*that the 490 years* (70 weeks of years) *are the first part of the 2300 years.* He began them synchronously, 453 years before the birth of Christ—terminating the 490 years in A.D. 37, and the 2300 years in 1847. . . . Soon men on both sides of the Atlantic, in Africa, even in India and other countries, began to set forth their convictions in similar vein" (*Questions*, 313).

Here is a fact that those who doubt Adventist doctrine must note: Our prophetic structure existed long before the Millerite movement. If our denomination is to be censured for our interpretations, so should the illustrious company of biblical scholars who gave us our prophetic heritage.

Chapter 7

Rehash
or Research?

(Updating Prophetic Interpretation—1)

It takes less faith now to become a Seventh-day Adventist than it did five years ago—at least in terms of believing our message. Recent world events have made the prophetic scenario we've anticipated for more than a century more plausible to any open-minded observer:

• The triumph of Desert Storm vaulted the United States to new heights of global leadership, where it can influence the world to worship the beast of Revelation 13. After Watergate and the Vietnam War, America's fortunes had fallen, and Communism's star was rising. Now, in the nineties, the tables have turned. The United States is back, standing tall as the world's only superpower. People everywhere are looking to the star-spangled banner for leadership in a "new world order."

• The pope has emerged as a major power broker in world affairs. Working closely with world political leaders, John Paul II is rapidly fulfilling his religiopolitical agenda in harmony with our prophetic expectations. The bombshell book by Jesuit scholar Malachi Martin, *The Keys of This Blood*, provides startling insight into the ambitions of the papacy. It dramatically vindicates another book written more than a century ago, our own *Great Controversy*.

• During the last several decades, many feared that a nuclear shootout between the superpowers might terminate life on this planet. The disintegration of the Soviet Union has reduced the chances of a global holocaust. More likely now is a smaller, regional blast on the scale of Hiroshima from a terrorist nation or breakaway republic. Such a limited nuclear event would allow life on earth to continue until the second coming of Christ, as Adventists have always said it would.

• With the demise of European Communism, doors are open to the gospel in ways that seemed impossible just five years ago. Adventists have enjoyed unique opportunities for evangelism in these newly liberated nations. It is becoming increasingly possible to preach the gospel in all the world so Jesus can come.

In addition to the incredible developments just listed, other pieces of the prophetic puzzle have been quietly fitting themselves into place. For example, in times of economic or military crisis, people willingly, even eagerly trade liberty for security. The world is facing a massive monetary meltdown, and it's just a matter of time before some warmonger lights the fuse that explodes the Middle East powder keg. So our days of freedom are numbered.

It isn't hard to discern the possibility of desperate political leaders eventually yielding to demands for a universal Sunday law and the ultimate death decree. Even now, right-wing reactionary forces are proposing repressive religious legislation as a solution for society's multiplying problems.

Amid all this, the Seventh-day Adventist Church is rapidly expanding around the globe. After the Ford and Davenport crises of the early eighties, some predicted that our church would split apart or be crippled permanently. Yet here we are, alive and well, gaining 2,000 new members every day. The Adventist family now includes more than seven million worldwide. Despite our many shortcomings, particularly in North America, God's truth goes marching on. Faithful members everywhere are preparing to fulfill their prophetic role of calling God's people out of Babylon.

REHASH OR RESEARCH?

What a time to be a Seventh-day Adventist! Of course, God has true believers in other churches, who are just as much His children as we are. However, other denominations languish in one of two traps—either they downplay Bible prophecy or they are entangled in the confusion of mistaken prophetic enthusiasm. The focal point of false prophecy is Jerusalem, where millions of Christians anticipate a rebuilt Jewish temple. Popular guru Hal Lindsey, in his bestselling *The Late Great Planet Earth*, predicts "there will be a reinstitution of the Jewish worship according to the law of Moses with sacrifices and oblations."[1] Imagine modern animal sacrifices being restored! Such an abomination would compete with Calvary and blaspheme the saving sacrifice of our Lord Jesus Christ, yet many Christians seem eager to welcome it as a spiritual revival.

The Adventist sanctuary message points away from any counterfeit temple on earth to heaven's sanctuary, where Jesus intercedes for us. Anything that glorifies the work of human hands in building a false temple must be a false teaching, a false prophecy.

It's really quite simple: True prophecy points upward to heaven's temple in the New Jerusalem, while false prophecy points downward to an earthly temple in old Jerusalem.

Thank God for the message of historic Adventism, which leads us to look to Jesus in His heavenly sanctuary. That's not to say we have never made mistakes in our prophetic interpretation. Remember, we grew out of the Great Disappointment of 1844. In the years immediately following, Sabbatarian Adventists believed that probation had already closed for the world at large and that only Millerites could still be saved.

Many church scholars now acknowledge that Ellen White herself mistakenly promoted belief in that "shut door." Then God enlightened her understanding of final events, to the great blessing of the church.

In this century, Adventists have continued to carry the prophetic torch the Lord placed in the hands of our pioneers. At times we've also made mistakes in our interpretations (nobody's perfect). For example, after World War II, many Adventists insisted that Israel would never establish itself as a nation in the

Middle East. They felt they had Scripture's support for such a position. Of course, Israel has emerged today as a significant military and political force in the Middle East.

Many Adventist evangelists were similarly embarrassed near the end of World War I. Referring to Daniel 11, they confidently predicted that the Turks would meet their demise after centuries of control over Palestine. But British general Allenby pushed north from Egypt and stopped that from happening.

We can take comfort from the fact that nothing Ellen White had written encouraged that misinterpretation. The source of the problem was Uriah Smith's book, *Daniel and the Revelation*. Smith performed a wonderful service for the church in his analysis of the prophecies, but it would be expecting too much to think his book contained no error. Some evangelists and scholars put too much confidence in Smith's interpretations, and they learned a lesson about skating on the thin ice of speculation.

So prudence regarding prophetic interpretation is commendable. But I'm wondering whether we've gone to the other extreme and become too cautious. While publicly proclaiming the tried and true, privately we ought to be constantly probing the Word for new insights relevant to changing world circumstances. Since putting Uriah Smith's Turkey to roost, unfortunately, most Adventists seem reluctant to reawaken investigation of prophecies such as those in Daniel chapters 11 and 12. Have we become fossilized in a nineteenth-century outlook?

Here in the 1990s the Seventh-day Adventist Church desperately needs relevance in our prophetic proclamation. We will not impress intelligent minds when we point to the 1755 Lisbon earthquake as a compelling sign of the times. That was important news in days gone by, but what about the twentieth century? I'm convinced that certain prophecies in both Daniel and other Old Testament books, along with Revelation, have much additional light for the end-time church.

Despite this, we seem content today with rehash rather than research. I sense a reluctance by some in the church to do serious research in Daniel and Revelation. Are we afraid of getting political blisters from handling prophetic hot potatoes?

Much of this concern is legitimate. Beyond avoiding the

public embarrassment that comes from mistaken positions, we must be wary of fanatics who grab a text here and a quotation there and cook up unlikely, unprovable assumptions that threaten our prophetic heritage. So let's be careful—yet not so fearful that we forfeit our responsibility to study the prophecies for ourselves.

I wonder whether some Adventists are frightened of learning something that Ellen White didn't know a century ago. For them, her prophetic gift has become a ball and chain preventing further advancement in their knowledge of the Word. The following quotation from the prophet's own pen could set them free:

No one must be permitted to close the avenues whereby the light of truth shall come to the people. As soon as this shall be attempted, God's Spirit will be quenched, for that Spirit is constantly at work to give fresh and increased light to His people through His Word.[2]

Fascinating thought—God is always seeking to reveal new light through the Bible. The grand old pillars remain unchanged, of course, and our historic prophetic platform stays intact. The heavenly millennium following the literal, visible coming of Christ, the 1844 judgment following the 2,300-year prophecy, and the 1,260 years of Daniel 7—these are eternal prophetic verities that will stand forever. But let's not be defensive about every jot and tittle of our pioneers' interpretations. More about this later.

Some Adventists pride themselves on not getting bogged down with the misinterpretations of our past, but they go to the other extreme and dismiss prophecy altogether. They don't preach it in public; they don't talk about it in private; and apparently they don't study it personally. All they seem to care about is whether people feel good about themselves and have meaningful relationships.

Self-esteem is important and so is getting along with others in this world here and now. But what about the future? Shouldn't we keep up our antennae regarding God's plans for this world and for us personally? We need to study Bible prophecy.

It helps to remember that prophecy isn't just a matter of abstract doctrine. It is of personal concern to you and me and the whole world because it gives us insights into where we will be next year, in the year 2000, and in eternity. So prophecy is vital to everyone, everywhere.

I am distressed at those Adventist secularists who not only ignore prophecy but even doubt God's ability to foretell the future. Some have suggested that God lacks foreknowledge, arguing that if He knew the future, that would somehow contradict human free will. Not true—the Bible makes it clear that God knows the end from the beginning while also letting individual souls decide their own destiny.

Nevertheless, many well-meaning church members wouldn't think of sponsoring a prophetic evangelistic crusade. Their community outreach is limited to health and family seminars and various compassion projects for the disadvantaged. Loving service toward our neighbors is a fulfilling of God's law, and we should do more than ever to help the homeless and to relieve human suffering in other ways. Let's remember, though, that this whole world will be a homeless wasteland after the second coming of Christ. The ultimate answer to human suffering is the good old blessed hope of going to heaven.

We must do more than pass out blankets to our neighbors on the sloping decks of the Titanic; we ought to point them to the prophecies of God's Word and warn them that this world is sinking rapidly. We ought to invite them to get on board the lifeboat of God's mercy and truth in Jesus Christ.

May God help us be more than Seventh-day Episcopalians, Sabbath keepers who have a social conscience but lack regard for the signs of the times. On the other hand, let's not be Seventh-day Traditionalists, mindlessly maintaining everything of our past, including mistaken interpretations.

Ellen White had the following warning for those who dig in their heels, refusing to search for additional truth:

A spirit of pharisaism has been coming in upon the people who claim to believe the truth for these last days. They are self-satisfied. They have said, "We have the truth. There is no more light for the people of God." But we are not safe when we take a position that we will not accept anything else than that upon which we have settled as truth. We should take *the Bible* and investigate it closely *for ourselves. . . .* There is no excuse for anyone in taking the position that there is no more truth to be revealed, and that all our expositions of Scripture are without an error. . . . There are those who oppose everything that is not in accordance with their own ideas, and by so doing they endanger their eternal interest as verily as did the Jewish nation in their rejection of Christ. . . . It was the unwillingness of the Jews to give up their long-established traditions that proved their ruin. They were determined not to see any flaw in their own opinions or in their expositions of the Scriptures. . . . *We have many lessons to learn, and many, many to unlearn. God and heaven alone are infallible.*[3]

An amazing quotation, I'd say. In light of it, I wish our church would convene a major Bible conference for the purpose of studying Daniel 11 and 12. It would be a week well spent. Our best scholars, responsible lay members, and pastors could examine those final chapters of Daniel with their mysterious 1,260, 1,290, and 1,335 days. What time spans do they represent?

I hope that nothing will keep us from mining the gold ore buried in Daniel 11 and 12. Please don't ask me what those mysterious time periods represent—I don't know. I have some ideas, but I'm trying to avoid undue speculation. The test of new light is whether it enhances or detracts from Christ and His established pillars of doctrine.

Well, so much for the book of Daniel. Let's move over to Revelation. I believe we find significant evidence in chapters 4 and 5 for the pre-advent judgment. Notice the striking similarity between these two chapters and Daniel 7:

Daniel 7		Revelation 4, 5
verse 9	Thrones Set	4:2
verse 9	God on the Throne	4:2
verses 9, 10	Description of Scene	4:3-6
verse 10	Myriads of Angels	5:11
verse 10	Books	5:2-9
verse 10	Opening of Books	5:2-9
verse 13	Jesus in Humanity	5:5
verse 13	Jesus Comes Before Throne	5:7
verse 14	Christ Receives Kingdom	5:12, 13
verse 22	Saints Favorably Accepted	5:9
verse 22	Saints Receive Kingdom	5:10

Some of these parallels seem especially compelling.[4] The connection between Daniel 7 and Revelation 4 and 5 is further confirmed as we notice three elements of judgment common to both passages:

Daniel 7

1. *God's rulership is vindicated* as Christ is "given dominion and glory and a kingdom" (verse 14).

2. *Satan's challenge is defeated*, for dominion is awarded to the Son of Man.

3. *The saints are vindicated*, for they "possess the kingdom" (verse 22).

Revelation 4 and 5

1. *God's rulership is vindicated* as with Christ He is ascribed "glory and dominion." "Worthy is the Lamb that was slain to receive power . . . and glory" (Revelation 5:13, 12, NASB).

2. *Satan's challenge is defeated*, for dominion is awarded to the Lamb.

3. *The saints are vindicated*, for the verdict of this judgment "made them to be a kingdom . . . and they will reign upon the earth" (Revelation 5:10, NASB).

To me, these parallel passages speak of a celestial judgment to occur *after* the cross but *before* the end of time.[5] This is vital

REHASH OR RESEARCH?

New Testament vindication of historic Adventism. I learned it back in 1980 during my quest to find a biblical base for my confidence in the Adventist sanctuary message. I can't tell you how much it has anchored my faith to realize that the book of Revelation describes the actual courtroom drama of heaven's pre-advent judgment. And the verdict announced there thrills my heart with gospel assurance: "Worthy is the Lamb!"

I believe the judgment scene of Revelation 4 and 5 is the cornerstone of the whole book. Everything preceding it builds up to that event. The first chapter establishes Christ's credentials as true Lord of this world in celestial majesty; the next two chapters prepare the churches for the judgment of chapters 4 and 5. And everything that follows chapter 5 in the book of Revelation comes out of the sanctuary once this cosmic pre-advent court reaches its verdict.

Come and see what I mean. First, the heavenly universe confirms God's right to rule: "The seventh angel sounded; and there arose loud voices in heaven, saying, 'The kingdom of the world has become the kingdom of our Lord, and of His Christ; and He will reign forever and ever'" (Revelation 11:15, NASB).[6]

Having been affirmed in His government, God then executes the verdict of the judgment. "We give Thee thanks . . . because Thou hast taken Thy great power and hast begun to reign" (verse 17, NASB). The time has come for "wrath" and "reward" (verse 18). "Then the temple of God was opened in heaven, and the ark of His covenant was seen in His temple. And there were lightnings, noises, thunderings, an earthquake, and great hail" (verse 19).

The saints share their Lord's victory over the enemy:

> Then I heard a loud voice saying in heaven, "Now salvation, and strength, and the kingdom of our God, and the power of His Christ have come, for the accuser of our brethren, who accused them before our God day and night, has been cast down. And they overcame him by the blood of the Lamb and by the word of their testimony, and they did not love their lives to the death" (Revelation 12:10, 11).

"Rejoice over her [Babylon], O heaven, and you saints and apostles and prophets, because God has pronounced judgment *for* you *against* her" (Revelation 18:20, NASB, emphasis supplied).

What's next? The seven last plagues come from "out of the temple" upon the wicked (Revelation 15:5, 6). This punishment is terrible, but the universe is convinced that "it is their just due" (Revelation 16:6). "Even so, Lord God Almighty, true and righteous are Your judgments" (verse 7). Finally comes a loud voice "out of the temple of heaven, from the throne, saying, 'It is done!'" (verse 17). All these climactic acts of the great controversy come from the sanctuary after God has been vindicated in the judgment of Revelation chapters 4 and 5.

This judgment weds Christ to His church: "'Alleluia! For the Lord God Omnipotent reigns! Let us be glad and rejoice and give Him glory, for the marriage of the Lamb has come, and His wife has made herself ready'" (Revelation 19:6, 7). Christ's family has been sealed to Him, and He has been sealed to them. Finally He can come to take them home: "Then I saw heaven opened, and behold, a white horse. And He who sat on him was called Faithful and True, and in righteousness He judges and makes war" (verse 11). The wicked are slain, and the devil, like the scapegoat on the ancient Day of Atonement, is exiled to the wilderness. God's people are transported to the "marriage supper of the Lamb" (verse 9).

So there, for what it's worth, is my brief overview of Revelation. What you just read may differ in some respects from our traditional understanding—yet it doesn't threaten any of our established doctrines. On the contrary, it bolsters confidence in the pre-advent judgment by acknowledging that historic pillar of faith. Tell me, haven't you ever wished that the pre-advent judgment would be explicitly and emphatically endorsed in the New Testament? Well, we may have it right there in the book of Revelation.

You might have been surprised to think that the seven seals and the trumpets can be seen as symbolizing events in the future rather than being fulfilled in past history. Don't worry, no doctrine has been threatened. On the contrary, our doctrines are confirmed.

For example, Revelation 9:4 says the fifth trumpet brings trouble upon those who "do not have the seal of God on their foreheads." If that happened hundreds of years ago, as Uriah Smith taught, it seems we have a serious problem convincing people that this seal of God on the forehead involves a future conflict over the Sunday law. Think about it.

There is a further problem about interpreting Revelation 9 in the past. Our current knowledge of medieval history casts doubt upon Smith's account of its past fulfillment. It makes more sense to defend our historic belief about the seal of God and the mark of the beast by seeing Revelation 9 as taking place in the future.

I don't claim to have all the answers, believe me. I'm mainly asking questions. But why should we blindly cling to the interpretations of Uriah Smith? We have everything to gain and nothing to lose by acknowledging the 1844 pre-advent judgment in Revelation 4 and 5 and the future Sabbath seal in Revelation 9.

Keep in mind that one of the key tests of any new interpretation of Scripture is whether it supports or undermines our established pillars of faith, particularly as stated in the church's twenty-seven points of fundamental belief. The key points of our faith that are affected by our interpretation of prophecy include the heavenly sanctuary, the investigative judgment, and the 2,300 days in Daniel and the Sabbath, the seal of God, and the mark of the beast in Revelation. On these there must be no compromise.

But there are still many new insights—new light if you please—to be gained from both Daniel and Revelation, which will not compromise our fundamental beliefs. In fact, we have much to learn that will *enhance* these key points of faith. As we move toward these new insights, we can expect to encounter disagreement. New views are difficult for some people, particularly when the new appears to contradict a cherished view of the past. But as long as there is no compromise of established truth, disagreement over interpretation, though painful at times, is a part of the process of discovering new truth.

MORE ADVENTIST HOT POTATOES

I hope everyone who claims to accept the ministry of Ellen White believes her when she says: "I have been shown that Jesus will reveal to us *precious old truths in a new light,* if we are ready to receive them; *but they must be received in the very way in which the Lord shall choose to send them.*"[7]

---

1. Hal Lindsey, *The Late Great Planet Earth* (New York: Bantam Books, 1979), 46.

2. Ellen White, quoted in LeRoy E. Froom, *Movement of Destiny* (Washington, D.C.: Review and Herald, 1971), 233.

3. Ellen White, *Counsels to Writers and Editors* (Nashville: Southern Publishing Association, 1946), 34-37.

4. Daniel 7:10 and Revelation 5:11 are the only places in the Bible that number the angels in this particular way. In fact, the New International Version gives identical wording. Also, the opening of books is symbolic of judgment (compare Daniel 7:10 with Revelation 20:11, 12). Both times Christ is presented as a member of the human family, which is significant because it's the humanity of Jesus that qualifies Him to defend us in the judgment, according to John 5:26, 27. In both passages Jesus comes before the throne to open the books—evidently He devotes a phase of His priestly ministry to judgment.

5. Notice the careful distinction in Revelation 4 and 5 between the timing of redemption and judgment. Redemption is *past*; judgment is *present*: "And they sang a new song, saying, 'You are worthy to take the scroll [*present*], and to open its seals [*present*]; for You were slain [*past*], and have redeemed us to God by Your blood [*past*]'" (Revelation 5:9). "The Root of David, has prevailed [*past*] to open the scroll [*present*] and to loose its seven seals" (Revelation 5:5).

There is clearly a separation between past redemption, accomplished at the cross, and a future time when Christ comes to the Father to open the book of judgment. All of this supports our doctrine of a celestial judgment after Calvary and before the second coming.

6. Similar acclamations regarding God's kingdom and His character are found throughout the book of Revelation following the judgment scene in chapters 4 and 5. See chapters 11:17; 12:10; 14:7; 15:3, 4; 16:5-7; 18:20; 19:1-7.

7. Ellen White, quoted in Froom, *Movement of Destiny*, 231.

Chapter 8

Fatima and
the Final Conflict

(Updating Prophetic Interpretation—2)

We Adventists have always had much to say about the Catholic Church regarding final events. And that's appropriate, since we believe Bible prophecy designates Rome as a major player in the course of final events. Have we ever stopped to wonder, though, what Catholics themselves think about the last days? What do they see on the prophetic horizon?

Catholics are not famous for their interest in prophecy, but millions of them have a devout fascination with a prophetic scenario that most Protestants have never heard of: the secrets of Fatima. Events connected with the Fatima revelations are as important to many Catholics as Sunday-law possibilities are to Adventists. We would do well to inform ourselves about what's going on in Catholicism's prophecy department and to discover the best scriptural response. In our search we will meet the King of the North, a controversial figure whose identity was once a prophetic hot potato in Adventist history.

Personally, for a long time I've wondered about Daniel 11's King of the North and his archrival, the King of the South. They are vitally involved in Daniel's most explicit reference to the time of trouble about to burst upon us. Despite the overwhelming relevance of Daniel chapters 11 and 12, most Adventists ignore them. As I mentioned a few pages back, this perplexes and frustrates me. Let's take a further look at the relevance of these two chapters in the context of what the Church of Rome expects will happen in the days ahead.

MORE ADVENTIST HOT POTATOES

The dramatic awakening of democracy and religion in Eastern Europe may have caught the world by surprise—but millions of Roman Catholics around the world have long been expecting a revival of religious freedom behind the former Iron Curtain. Their confidence is based upon something that happened on May 13, 1917, outside the town of Fatima, Portugal.

On that day, according to the popular account, three shepherd children were tending their flock when, around noontime, they suddenly saw a flash of lightning, although the day was clear. Frightened, they turned to flee. Just then, the image of a beautiful young woman appeared to them. This supernatural apparition later identified itself as the virgin Mary. During six separate appearances to the children, the virgin disclosed specific information of profound importance regarding the future of the world and the Catholic Church.

Have you ever heard about these appearances at Fatima? Even Adventists are surprisingly unaware of the regard millions of Catholics have for them. Many books and articles have been written about Fatima, including an Emmy Award–winning film hosted by actor Ricardo Montalban. Some Catholic scholars have actually said that what happened at Fatima is the most significant spiritual event of this century.

What is the message of Fatima? Some of it remains a secret to this day, but much is known of what the shepherd children reported hearing. I've gleaned the following from a dozen different Catholic sources, including Malachi Martin's recent book, *The Keys of This Blood*.

"The war [World War I] will finally end," the children reported hearing. "However, if people do not cease offending God, a worse war will break out, and God will punish the world for its crimes by means of war, famine, and persecution of the church and the Holy Father.

"If people do not stop offending God, Russia will spread errors throughout the world, and the good will be martyred. Several nations will be annihilated, but in the end, Russia will be converted and a certain period of peace will be granted the world."

Then came a special secret for the pope alone. No pontiff has ever revealed it publicly, but insiders at the Vatican confide that it predicts a calamity through which God will work to bring the world to its knees in repentance. This calamity might also be accompanied by an attempt upon the pope's life.

All this amounted to quite a solemn warning for three children to communicate. The apparition of Mary promised to return and clarify the messages. She also instructed the children that five months later, on October 13, a dramatic public miracle would verify the messages.

The prediction came true. Many newspapers reported that on October 13, 1917, an expectant crowd of 70,000 to 80,000 witnessed a miracle involving a gyrating movement of the sun that lasted twelve minutes. Other parts of Fatima's prophecy have been fulfilled beyond question. Russia certainly did become a world power, spreading its errors of atheism around the world. And there was indeed another world war, worse than the first, just as predicted. In January 1939, a mysterious light is reported to have illuminated the night sky in part of Europe. This happened after another warning from the Fatima apparition. Then came World War II.

In recent times, the most dramatic event connected with Fatima was the attempted assassination of Pope John Paul II. It happened on May 13, 1981—the sixty-fourth anniversary of the reported appearance at Fatima. Since then, the pontiff has frequently commented on the coincidence of the 1917 vision and the assassination attempt both occurring on May 13.

On May 13, 1982, precisely one year after the attempt upon his life, John Paul made a pilgrimage to the town of Fatima. Surrounded by a crowd of one-and-a-half million worshipers, he praised the lady of Fatima for saving his life.

What's next, according to the Fatima timetable? Many Catholic scholars predict that the dramatic developments between the Vatican and the Kremlin are just the first steps of more to come. They believe Russia will actually become converted to Christianity. To pave the way, according to the prophecy of Fatima, the pope must make a specific, public appeal for the conversion of Russia. After that, the miracle will not be long in coming. This is what millions of Catholic Christians believe will happen soon—very soon.

MORE ADVENTIST HOT POTATOES

The conversion of the Russian empire would be dramatic but not unprecedented. Was not the ancient Roman empire "Christianized" by the church? One thing seems certain—Fatima's blueprint for Russia is far more plausible than it was five years ago.

Seeking further information, I contacted Jean Whalen, a devout Catholic and a national leader in enthusiasm for Fatima. The general consensus among Catholics, she told me, is that the promised Russian conversion hasn't happened yet. This is a time to wait and see when the pope will make a public appeal for bishops everywhere to pray for the conversion of Russia.

Jean Whalen told me that in 1984 Pope John Paul II did make a general appeal in a letter to the bishops to pray for the conversion of the world. What needs to happen, she said, is that he make a specific appeal for the Christianization of Russia. He is said to be postponing that for now, not wanting to antagonize Russian authorities.

A serious relationship between the Kremlin and the Vatican began a couple of years ago with the historic meeting in Rome between Pope John Paul and Mikhail Gorbachev, then president of what used to be the Soviet Union. It was the first face-to-face encounter between the leaders of these two world powers. They talked alone in Russian, later calling in their aides. The meeting lasted well over an hour, after which came several announcements. John Paul publicly endorsed *perestroika*, Gorbachev's attempt to restructure Soviet society. Gorbachev then opened the door to diplomatic relations with the Vatican and mentioned the possibility of the pontiff visiting the Soviet Union. John Paul didn't immediately accept the invitation, perhaps waiting to see if Gorbachev would keep his promise of providing full freedom to Soviet Catholics.

The evening before his meeting with the pope, Gorbachev had shocked reporters by openly stating his nation's need for spiritual values. He further affirmed that government should never interfere with an individual's right to religious liberty.

Incredible words, which set the stage for Gorbachev's meeting with the pope the next day. The two leaders came out of the papal library looking like familiar friends.

Just a year earlier, few observers of world affairs would have imagined that such a meeting would be possible. Yet this peace conference between the Kremlin and the Vatican crowned an eleven-year effort by the pope to achieve religious freedom for his parishioners behind the Iron Curtain.

In 1978, when the Polish cardinal Karol Wojtyla became Pope John Paul II, the church was suffering Communist oppression. The new pontiff quietly determined to spark a change. Eight months after assuming office, he made a papal visit to his homeland. Massive crowds cheered his expression of religious faith and Polish patriotism. He proclaimed himself "this Slav, this Pole," who was working to preserve "the spiritual unity of Christian Europe." In an unmistakable challenge to the country's atheistic government, John Paul appealed for his fellow Poles to maintain their Christian heritage.

The pope returned to Rome but not before stirring up sufficient national spirit in Poland to give birth to the Solidarity labor union. When the government condemned this direct threat to authoritarian rule, the pope brought Lech Walesa and a delegation of Solidarity members to the Vatican. There he explicitly and emphatically endorsed their bold adventure in freedom.

That might have been too much for his atheistic enemies. Not long afterward came the assassination attempt upon the pope's life. Investigators concluded that the would-be assassin did not act alone. A trail of evidence linked him to Eastern European Communists. Although the association was never established beyond question, certainly the motivation was clear—to silence the one man capable of shaking the foundations of international Communism.

John Paul recovered and resumed his warfare against atheistic Communism. A few months later, the crisis in Poland came to a climax when the government declared martial law. Troops massed for battle; a bloody civil war seemed imminent. Rumor has it the pope told the Communist government that if its Soviet troops invaded Poland, he would immediately fly there and take his stand with his freedom-loving countrymen. The invasion never came.

During the next nineteen months of crisis, the pope frequently made public reference about his concern for Poland. He also gave private encouragement to Solidarity members while urging them to be patient and moderate in their demands.

Only the pope could harness the raw energy of Lech Walesa and his fellow reformers. Ever so gradually, the Kremlin came to recognize the Vatican as a moderating influence. So it was that the government allowed another visit from John Paul to his homeland. It was a further triumphant display of religious patriotism, more powerful than ever.

Each year the pope's position behind the Iron Curtain became stronger. In 1987, during yet another trip to Poland, John Paul publicly proclaimed support for the anti-government labor union. Before a cheering crowd he endorsed the word *solidarity* as a symbol of national pride.

During the 1988 strike at the Lenin Shipyard in Gdansk, when violence seemed about to break out, the pope did much to defuse the crisis. Speaking over Vatican radio, he calmed the agitated workers while at the same time communicating his support. Thanks to his intervention, the strike ended with a minimum of violence four days later. It was now obvious that the Soviet Union needed the pontiff to maintain law and order amid the awakening revolution.

In 1989 a Roman Catholic, Tadeusz Mazowiecki, a friend of Solidarity leader Lech Walesa, became Poland's first non-Communist prime minister since the end of World War II. One of his first official acts was to place a phone call to the pope, the man who had done more than anyone else to make it possible.

From Poland, the wildfire of freedom spread throughout Eastern Europe and into the former Soviet Union itself. Without question, the driving human force behind the revolutions of 1989 was the pope. When many others seemed to give up hope during the days of martial law in Poland in 1981, he inspired the spark of Solidarity to rise from prison to parliament. Emboldened by the decade-long example of the pope's beloved Solidarity, one by one the peoples of Eastern Europe awakened and moved their dream along. And the Soviet Union itself has now been revolutionized by democratic forces.

One wonders what the future will indeed hold, whether there will be a general conversion of Russia, as foretold at Fatima. The bombshell book *The Keys of This Blood* brought Fatima to the attention of many Adventists. No one can deny that the prophecy has been strikingly fulfilled so far. Evidently the devil is working to fulfill his own plans for this world, taking advantage of the open door in Russia. These astonishing and completely unexpected events do not in the least move us away from our historic prophetic platform. Instead, we have new insight into the prophetic role Rome sees for itself.

Will events in Jerusalem play a part in the counterfeit prophecies of Fatima? As far as I know, the revelations mentioned nothing about Jerusalem, but other popular scenarios do. As noted in the last chapter, many misguided Christians are eager to see the Jews rebuild their temple in Jerusalem in order to prepare the way for Christ to return. They believe such a temple will be built at the site of the golden Dome of the Rock. Jews cherish this spot as supremely sacred because their ancestors worshiped there in Solomon's temple. After its destruction by the Babylonian army, another temple replaced it, only to be destroyed in turn by the Romans after the time of Christ. With the temple and their holy city in ruins after A.D. 70, Jews scattered all over the world. At last, several years after World War II, Jewish people returned to Palestine to resume their own government. During the Six-Day War of 1967, they recaptured Jerusalem.

Many Israelis believe God gave Jerusalem back to them so they could erect a third temple. When temple services resume, they believe, the Messiah will set up His kingdom of glory there. So a rebuilt temple on this mount would fulfill the dreams of both Jews and Christians all over the world.

There's a major obstacle, though. Muslims control the Temple Mount. In fact, the Dome of the Rock is one of Islam's most sacred shrines too! Muslims believe Abraham offered his son to Allah on the holy rock beneath the dome. They also say that Mohammed ascended to heaven from that very rock. No wonder Muslims around the world would do anything to keep the Israelis from erecting a temple there.

Jews, however, regard the present Muslim occupation of the Temple Mount to be blasphemous. The Jewish temple on that site contained the Holy of Holies. To Jews, understandably, the Islamic mosque on the Temple Mount is an abomination.

There's no human hope for resolving the crisis. Since both Jews and Muslims stake a divine claim to the Temple Mount, someone's holy place is desecrated, no matter what happens.

The end-time expectations of three world religions point to the Temple Mount. Earth's final military conflict might well be a battle for its possession. Could this be the military focus of the spiritual battle of Armageddon?

All this talk about rebuilding the Jewish temple is setting up the world for a counterfeit Armageddon. The attention showered on Israel is a diversion of the enemy to confuse sincere Christians about the real issues of Bible prophecy.

The book of Daniel predicts that end-time tribulation will come in the context of a struggle between the King of the North and the King of the South. Uriah Smith wrote that Turkey was the King of the North. James White disagreed, saying it was the papacy. The matter became a prophetic hot potato in the Adventist Church back then. As it turned out, Smith's position resulted in the embarrassment, during World War I, discussed in the previous chapter.

I believe James White was correct. The King of the North in Daniel 11:36 is the same as the papal power in Daniel 8:11, 25. Additionally, long ago in Daniel's day, the King of the North was Babylon. Today Babylon represents Christianity fallen from grace, headquartered in Rome. Indeed, the pope has emerged as a world leader with enormous political influence, especially with NATO governments. Therefore, I believe that the King of the North represents a coalition willing to wage war in the name of Jesus, under the spiritual banner of the pope and the military leadership of the United States.

Who, then, is the King of the South? In Daniel's time it was Egypt. Remember, it was Pharaoh who scorned the existence of God: "Who is the Lord, that I should obey His voice to let Israel go? I do not know the Lord" (Exodus 5:2). The modern counterpart could be Islamic forces allied with leftover Communists. Muslims refuse to acknowledge the God of Christianity, even regarding all Christians as infidels. Militant Islamic govern-

110

ments suppress and actually outlaw Christian evangelism. They also present the greatest threat to the "new world order" President Bush loves to talk about.

Communism has been crumbling in recent years, although China—the most populous nation on earth—is still sworn to Marxism. Communist China provides militant Islamic nations with Silkworm missiles and other weaponry. As for Communism in the former Soviet Union, it's still possible that reactionary hard-liners of the type that staged the ill-fated coup against President Gorbachev will succeed in causing havoc in their fragmenting nation. Suppose right-wing elements of the army get control of some nuclear weapons. They would pose a real threat to world peace.

If Russia is "Christianized" in harmony with the Fatima prediction and joins with the "King of the North," atheistic military elements in that country could resist and cause incalculable risk to regional and global stability. Then, suppose this desperate, last-gasp thrust of Communism threatens the newly liberated nations of Eastern Europe—particularly Catholic Poland. Western Christian forces under the influence of the pope would find it hard to resist coming to their defense. It is not difficult to imagine a life-and-death struggle between atheistic forces and a coalition of counterfeit Christianity.

I'm not saying that this is how the battle between the King of the North and the King of the South is going to happen. I'm just suggesting a possible scenario that seems to me to harmonize the current geopolitical situation with the prophetic expectations of historic Adventism.

Where would non-Christian Eastern countries, such as India, fit in? What about tribal Africa? We can expect these countries to march under the banner of the pope, who has positioned himself as the religious leader of east as well as west. In the West, New Age adherents also find themselves increasingly comfortable with the compromised, partially paganized Christianity that Rome represents.

What about Israel? Although certainly not a Christian power, the Israelis align themselves with the military, political, and financial sponsorship of Western Christian governments. Remember, the basic philosophy of Middle East relationships is this: the enemy of my enemy is my friend. Since militant Islam has made itself the mortal enemy of both Christianity and Judaism, the latter groups are friends. Beyond that, since apostate Christianity anticipates a rebuilt Jewish temple in Jerusalem as its blessed hope, it welcomes Israel as a partner in the King-of-the-North federation.

Let's pause to summarize now. Prophecy calls for the United States to provide military and political leadership for the interests of Rome. The only military forces in the world today that pose a threat to the United States are those of militant Muslims and leftover Communists. So it seems reasonable to expect a colossal end-time military showdown between a coalition favorable to apostate Christianity (the King of the North) against forces hostile to Christianity (the King of the South). Earth's final military conflict might stem from a showdown in Jerusalem between the physical descendants of Abraham: the children of Ishmael fighting the children of Isaac and their allies—militant Muslims and their friends against Judeo-Christian forces.

Who will overcome? According to Daniel 11, initially the King of the North is successful. Then comes an unexpected setback. The King of the North, returning from defeat, will be "enraged at the holy covenant and take action" (Daniel 11:30, NASB). This could be Babylon's attempt to secure God's help through passing religious legislation—national salvation by law, the ultimate legalism.

Verse 31 says Babylon will "defile the sanctuary . . . and place there the abomination of desolation." Is this the Sunday law we have anticipated?

Ultimately, the whole earth will join forces against God's faithful remnant: "I saw three unclean spirits like frogs coming out of the mouth of the dragon, out of the mouth of the beast, and out of the mouth of the false prophet. For they are spirits of demons, performing signs, which go out to the kings of the earth and of the *whole world*, to gather them to the battle of that great day of God Almighty" (Revelation 16:13, 14, emphasis supplied).

So the devil's all-star team will be the dragon, the beast, and the false prophet. The dragon is paganism with its outright connection with the devil (see Revelation 12:9), along with the host of New Age delusions. The beast, of course, is the papal system. The false prophet is apostate Protestantism, which lays false claim to the Word of God in "sola Scriptura." The "whole world" will come under the compelling influence of evil spirits. This would include Communist and Muslim nations. Convinced by the satanic supershow of miracles, everyone will ultimately accept conversion to counterfeit worship. So sooner or later, the Fatima prophecy of Russia's conversion will apparently be fulfilled. Everyone but the remnant will honor the beast and receive his mark.

Notice that these evil spirits will come out of the *mouths* of the miracle-working deceivers. What moves within a mouth? The tongue. And these spirits are described as froglike. What is the outstanding feature of a frog? His tongue. Could it be the tongues of a false Pentecost that will unite the world?

One cannot prove such a conclusion about tongues explicitly from the text, but one might see speaking in tongues implied there—the fact is that the evil spirits are likened to frogs, and frogs do catch their prey with their tongues.

Now back to Daniel 11. God takes advantage of hatred against the truth to give the loud cry, the final gospel proclamation in strength: "Those who do wickedly against the covenant he [the King of the North] shall corrupt with flattery; but the people who know their God shall be strong, and carry out great exploits" (Daniel 11:32).

Thank God, we will not be defenseless in that final crisis. He will be our refuge and strength, a very present help in a "time of trouble such as never was since there was a nation, even to that time" (Daniel 12:1).

"Many shall be purified, made white, and refined" (verse 10). Then at last the purpose of God will be accomplished. The announcement goes forth about the remnant: "Here is the patience of the saints; here are those who keep the commandments of God and the faith of Jesus" (Revelation 14:12).

For this remnant God has been waiting a long time. May He not have to wait much longer.

Chapter 9

Have Our Hospitals Lost Their Way?

(Adventist Health System)

Every church institution has its problems, and doubtless Loma Linda University Medical Center is no exception. But I gained a new appreciation for that institution in February 1991, when I travelled there with a production team to tape a documentary about well-known Adventists for viewing overseas.

One person we interviewed was Dr. Leonard Bailey. Amid his crowded schedule of surgeries and consultations, he took time to explain his pioneering accomplishments in the field of infant heart transplants. I was particularly impressed with his soft-spoken humility, wondering whether I could survive the glare of media attention as well as he apparently has.

Next, we visited Dr. James Slater and the proton beam accelerator, a massive lifesaving unit designed to irradiate cancerous tumors with minimal damage to surrounding tissue. Again we witnessed humility from a Loma Linda physician who combines world-class expertise with warm-hearted concern for hurting people.

On that mild winter day, our production team spent an hour outdoors interviewing Dr. Joan Coggin of the Loma Linda heart team. Joan is one of the most delightful people I've ever met; I cherish her as a friend. Once more, we all were impressed with an Adventist physician's integrity, caring, and concern.

Afterward, we went to the office of Dr. Lyn Behrens, president of the university. As she articulated the goals and programs of Loma Linda, I felt proud to be associated with this flagship of the Adventist Health System (AHS).

Our production team, which included non-Adventists, came away from Loma Linda profoundly impressed with what we had witnessed—not just the technology and architecture, but the capable, compassionate medical staff there.

Of course, not all of our more than 600 health-care facilities can perform the advanced research or offer the services available at Loma Linda. Yet many shine in their own sphere with faithfulness and distinction. Where would the Adventist Church be without our hospitals? All over the world they serve as an "opening wedge" for the gospel, overcoming prejudice and winning confidence.

In North America we have many health-care institutions that are shining lights of spiritual compassion, moral integrity, and financial responsibility. Others have serious problems that need to be addressed.

Critics both within the church and without have made a hot potato out of the real and imaginary shortcomings of the Adventist Health System. Some assert that our hospitals have lost their way in worldliness. Is that true? What's wrong about our health-care system—and what's right about it?

Seeking to be accurate and fair in this analysis, I asked a friend, who is president of one of our hospitals, to take a brief questionnaire to a regional meeting of fellow AHS administrators. The survey listed a number of criticisms that have been leveled at our health-care system and asked the administrators to specify which criticisms they felt were valid and which were unfair. It also asked them to make suggestions for any necessary remedial actions.

That regional AHS headquarters declined to respond to my survey. A vice-president said they preferred to direct me to their own sources of information, which they felt sure could provide me with all the data I wanted. While I appreciated this offer of assistance, I decided it would be better to conduct my own interviews at the grass-roots level.

So I talked with a number of sources who have firsthand

information regarding our hospitals: physicians, nurses, hospital administrators both active and retired, other salaried AHS employees, hospital board members, pastors, and informed laypeople. I admit that the time constraints of a publication deadline have limited somewhat the data I've collected, so this chapter will not cover the range and depth I originally envisioned. Please understand also that this chapter is not a scientific study of our health system. It is a compilation of my personal observations and conclusions—just like the rest of this book.

Now, if you'll agree that these disclaimers don't disqualify me from conducting this discussion, let's move ahead.

One major concern I ran across in my interviews is the perception that many of our hospitals are losing their spiritual sense of mission. Yes, they offer the finest in medical care, people told me, but sometimes they make that an exclusive end in itself.

For example, chaplains in our hospitals sometimes offer professional encouragement and general spiritual comfort without seeming to have much interest in referring interested patients to pastors for follow-up after their recovery. Certainly a hospital is not the place for aggressive witnessing—that would be totally insensitive and counterproductive. But if chaplains and nurses are allowed and encouraged to take a simple spiritual interest in what happens to their patients after they leave the hospital, much more could be accomplished for the kingdom of God than is happening now.

I know of some hospitals where nurses are *not* supposed to initiate prayer with patients, even when they sense it would be welcome. The question must be asked: If we find it necessary to neglect the spiritual opportunities connected with patient care, why does the Adventist Church operate hospitals?

Another concern that came up as I talked with people is the feeling that many of our health-care institutions seem almost embarrassed about being Adventist-sponsored. They want so much to fit in with the community that they diminish or even delete their denominational identity. In too many Adventist hospitals, Sabbath seems just like any other day. On that day, at least, couldn't some quiet Christian music be playing in the lobby?

MORE ADVENTIST HOT POTATOES

Non-Adventist dietitians employed in our hospitals sometimes have little knowledge or interest in the unique diet the Lord has given this church. Of course, patients who prefer a meat menu should have it, but wouldn't many be open to learn a better way to eat if dietitians took an interest in helping them?

Do you see what I'm saying? While we certainly don't want to impose the Adventist lifestyle on patients, at least we could make it available.

This brings us to a personnel problem suffered by many of our hospitals. There simply are not enough Adventist nurses and physicians to fill staff positions. While it's perfectly proper to offer openings to nonmember employees (equal opportunity laws even require it), we must have sufficient Adventists on the staffs of our institutions to maintain our unique Adventist witness. If we expand to the point that we must dilute our Adventist presence, what are we accomplishing?

I want to emphasize that these problems with Adventist health care are by no means universal. Many of our hospitals manage to maintain an Adventist influence that is both uncompromised and compassionate. Still, I have to ask: Is the Adventist Health System straying from its medical-missionary mandate? We must decide a fundamental issue: Should the primary goal of our medical work be providing acute care, such as emergency services and surgery? Or should our major emphasis be health education and disease prevention, fostering a wholesome lifestyle for body and soul, with the ultimate goal of life eternal through Jesus Christ?

Let's take a look at the roots of our health system. Loma Linda University was originally established as the College of Medical Evangelists, commissioned to prepare missionary doctors and nurses for foreign and domestic service. Lately the balance has shifted from medical evangelism to advanced medical training. At one point, the university voted to phase out its School of Public Health. I've talked with faculty members who were deeply distressed about that decision. They challenged the assurance that the School of Medicine can provide adequate attention to health-education training. Thank God, the School of Public Health has now been preserved.

HAVE OUR HOSPITALS LOST THEIR WAY?

One doctor at Loma Linda University confided to me his doubts that we should have built the proton beam accelerator with its staggering cost of more than forty million dollars. Yes, he admitted, much of the funding came from outside sources, but it still involved a tremendous financial investment of our own. "Certainly society needs that machine," he said. "I'd be thankful for it myself if I had a brain tumor—but let someone else build it who doesn't have the health-evangelism heritage we seem to be abandoning." He concluded, "Mark my words, in order to make that machine cost-effective, they are going to have to run it on the Sabbath."

This doctor sounded quite convincing, until I remembered that Jesus did routine healing on the Sabbath. Why would it be wrong for the proton beam machine to operate on the day over which He is Lord? Elective treatment for patients not in pain is traditionally postponed on the Sabbath, and that's definitely the way it should be. However, if there is such a backload of patients with terminal tumors that people might die if the machine didn't run seven days a week, is it really breaking the Sabbath to offer such treatment?

I also think of a meeting I had with Dr. Slater, in which he expressed his hope of saving lives with the help of that huge machine. Whether Loma Linda University should have let someone else build the accelerator, I'm not qualified to say. I'm just thankful the proton beam is out there, rescuing people from deadly cancer.

It's so easy to criticize those who are trying to do good. Since the groundbreaking Baby Fae case, Dr. Leonard Bailey has endured much misunderstanding for performing infant heart transplants. Ethicists can debate the matter day and night, but think of the dozens of children alive today because of a transplanted heart from Loma Linda. If you were the parent of one of those children snatched from certain death, could you criticize what Loma Linda is doing?

On this matter of criticism, the Adventist Health System has come under fire for debts incurred in expansion and development. When I brought this up to one hospital president, he pointed out that the debt ratio for his institution is computed on the *original* purchase price, which is only half of the property's present value. So his debt ratio is only half as serious as it seems and well within acceptable limits.

That made sense to me, although I'm not a financial expert. I do know that the volatile real-estate market has turned many normally sound investments into disasters. The health-care industry has been especially hard hit, and certain Adventist institutions have not escaped trouble. In some cases, unwise decisions no doubt caused problems.

Everyone knows it's best to avoid debt whenever possible, yet sometimes loans are necessary. So let's not be too quick to criticize administrators in our institutions or conferences who find themselves forced to make high-risk financial decisions. Pray for them instead, and share with them your input.

Yet I must say that some things are happening at a few of our hospitals that I believe deserve not just criticism but outright censure. Such things as serving alcohol at community fund-raising dinners—a charge so serious I checked it out with the North American Division Health and Temperance Department. If that's what we must do to keep a hospital running, may the Lord help us shut it down! Let's sell the place and get out of there rather than betray the ABCs of holy living!

One of the most controversial decisions of recent years involving the Adventist Health System is the decision to remunerate administrators according to community wage scales. In some regions of the country, annual salaries of top administrators in Adventist health-care institutions have swelled to more than $100,000. The rationale for this is fear that if we don't pay our leaders what secular hospital executives are getting, they will quit their jobs, and we will lose their services.

If such is the case, how have we managed through the years to find administrators willing and able to staff our health-care system? At the Adventist Media Center I know several employees whose specialized talents could bring them as much money as any hospital administrator could earn. One had been a successful commercial television producer. Several times a year this man hires a professional production team to help him shoot a series of telecasts for our media center. One freelance assistant under his direction earns $100 an hour, which works out to more than $200,000 annually. Our staffer gets only a fraction of that from standard denominational wages, yet I've never heard him complain about it or threaten to leave.

What keeps him from heading down to Hollywood? The answer is simple. He loves the Lord. He works for a nonprofit organization and has some sense of sacrifice.

Yet no matter how strongly we may feel that something is amiss in this matter of remuneration, we must resist the temptation to denounce Adventist health-care administrators who receive huge salaries. What do we know about how they are spending all that money? Maybe they are supporting an orphanage somewhere. Let God be the judge; we don't know individual circumstances.

I know of one administrator who earns $120,000 a year in the Adventist Health System. A lot of money, indeed. Yet when he accepted denominational employment he took a $40,000 pay *cut* from his previous position! Then he promptly used his considerable expertise to secure nine million dollars in available funding that the hospital hadn't known about. You can understand his perplexity when he lamented, "When I used to get $160,00 a year in the corporate world, everybody at church treated me with respect. Now they criticize me."

Hearing a story like that puts another perspective on this matter of wages. Even so, when all the facts are in, I still can't agree that we ought to pay committed Christian administrators six-figure salaries to retain their services. Think it through. If you pay hospital executives huge wages, then what about educators, publishing house leaders, computer experts, media specialists, and other high-octane employees? Suppose pastors with doctorates demanded wages commensurate with their training and expertise. Where do you draw the line? Have we not set a dangerous precedent that could sabotage the entire denominational wage structure?

When Jesus called the disciples to follow Him, He didn't offer them remuneration based on the community wage scale for religious leaders in Jerusalem. And, of course, one did become dissatisfied with the arrangement, judging his professional skills worthy of better compensation than other Christian workers. You know who he was and what happened to him.

I wonder how the Sisters of Mercy manage to run their hospitals on less than a community wage scale. Are Adventist administrators less dedicated than their peers in Catholic health care? I don't think so. I believe if we paid them a decent living wage they would be happy to serve just the same. Most of them, anyway. If anybody needs greener pastures than we can offer, let them go their way. In case everybody bails out, we could just close down the hospitals, sell them, and invest the proceeds in genuine medical-missionary evangelism.

Now we must address an area that worries me a lot. I'm talking about abortions performed at some of our hospitals. Thank God, many Adventist health-care institutions disallow abortion in all but extreme circumstances. For example, the policy at one of our largest hospitals states: "Termination of pregnancy for socioeconomic reasons is prohibited."

Some of our hospitals, however, are quite permissive in interpreting the church's present abortion guidelines. This brings concern to many members. Delegates at a Potomac Conference constituency meeting in September 1991 voted by an overwhelming majority to request that two local Adventist hospitals strictly limit the abortions performed there. By a margin of 190-58, delegates passed the following resolution appealing to the hospitals in that conference to:

Immediately adopt and implement abortion policies that institutionally prohibit abortions for social or economic reasons including convenience, birth control, gender selection, or avoidance of embarrassment; limiting the abortion procedure to those times when a pregnancy threatens the mother's physical life, when the fetus is gravely abnormal, and in cases of rape and incest. The appointment of a committee charged with prospectively reviewing all requests for abortion would be essential to ensure implementation of these guidelines.

We further ask the Abortion Study Commission to continue monitoring the abortion policies and numbers of abortions performed at our hospitals and to report to our next constituency meeting on the hospitals' response to this appeal. The committee shall consist of at least 50 percent female representation.

The meeting was an outgrowth of an unresolved discussion at a previous constituency meeting in 1987. Two years earlier, a local Adventist hospital had been the target of an abortion protest organized by a nearby evangelical church. Its pastor was quoted in the *Washington Post* as saying, "We find it very inconsistent for a hospital run by a Christian church to be practicing murder of unborn children."

Various area Adventists, alarmed by such a serious allegation, launched their own investigation of the hospital's abortion policy. Regarding such an explosive moral issue, they decided that Potomac members had the responsibility to provide input to hospitals bearing the name of their church within their conference territory.

Delegates wrestled with apparent discrepancies between abortion limits recommended in a 1970 church policy statement and a more liberal guideline adopted in 1971. Under the authority of the latter statement, a number of Adventist hospital boards apparently felt obliged to permit what some conference constituency delegates described as "abortion on demand."

It was quite a discussion that day, with both sides freely expressing their points and counterpoints. Some delegates urged respect for a woman's right to control what happens within her own body. Others responded that one person's right to choose ends where another's body begins and that no human should stop a heart from beating with the life of God.

Defenders of abortion insisted that our hospitals must not withhold a legal service from the community. Opponents argued that Adventist institutions have both the option and the responsibility to serve as a moral lighthouse to the community. "Adventists have never been silent about comparative trifles, such as makeup and amusements," one pastor's wife observed. "Surely we can stand up and be counted regarding the greatest moral issue of our time."

MORE ADVENTIST HOT POTATOES

Women delegates frequently stepped to the microphones to voice their convictions. One nurse defended "safe" hospital abortions by describing a teenager's trauma from an illegal "back-alley" operation. A pastor's wife told about the depression and remorse of many mothers whose abortions were legal.

So the discussion wore on as debate lasted though the afternoon. The conclusive argument, some thought, was that God is the Life-giver, and He wants Adventist hospitals to conduct the ministry of healing human life—not the abortion of it.

I personally hope that Adventists everywhere will enter into dialogue with AHS administrators about local abortion policies. Many of these administrators welcome input from church members, and we should let them know our convictions.

There you have my analysis of the Adventist Health System. As with all human institutions, our hospitals have their problems. Let's thank them for the good they are doing and pray for them where they fall short.

AN ELEVENTH-HOUR WAKE-UP CALL TO GOD'S SLEEPING ARMY

A storm is coming. But despite the sound of distant thunder, most don't know what's ahead.

In *The Crisis of the End Time*, Marvin Moore suggests that history's climax is about to break upon us with startling speed and ferocity. He also shows how we can keep our relationship with Jesus during earth's darkest hour.

The Crisis is a forceful yet easy-to-understand explanation of the vital issues facing our church and our world on the eve of Christ's return.

US$10.95/Cdn$13.50. Paper.

THE Crisis OF THE End Time

Marvin Moore

To order, call TOLL FREE **1-800-765-6955** (in the U.S.), or visit your local ABC.

Prices subject to change without notice.

The sanctuary, the judgment, and your salvation.

The sanctuary is one of the most misunderstood of our doctrines. Was it developed as a cover for the great disappointment in 1844? Does it have any bearing at all on our salvation?

In his most significant book to date, Clifford Goldstein establishes the relevance of the sanctuary and the investigative judgment to our salvation, our knowledge of God, and to our purpose as a people.

False Balances restores meaning to the phrase "present truth."

US$12.95/Cdn$15.55. Hardcover.

To order, call TOLL FREE: 1-800-765-6955 (in the U.S.), or visit your local ABC.

Prices subject to change without notice.

It's time we started talking about the things that really matter.

"Unless your righteousness exceeds that of the scribes and Pharisees..."

The pursuit of sinlessness has caused untold guilt, anxiety, and unscriptural extremism among many Adventists.

The Pharisee's Guide to Perfect Holiness re-examines what the Bible teaches about sin and salvation and puts the good news back into the gospel. Author George Knight grapples with what it really means to be "holy," how to be "like" Jesus, and what God does *for* us and *in* us.

This landmark book will resharpen your focus on God's amazing grace without blurring your view of His power over sin.

US$14.95/Cdn$17.95. Paper.

Available now at your local ABC, or simply order by phone! Call TOLL FREE: 1-800-765-6955 (in the U.S.). Prices subject to change without notice.

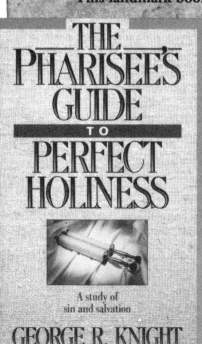

THE PHARISEE'S GUIDE TO PERFECT HOLINESS

A study of sin and salvation

GEORGE R. KNIGHT